The Folklore of the British Isles
General Editor: Venetia J. Newall

The Folklore of
The Isle of Man

The Folklore of The Isle of Man

Margaret Killip

Drawings by Norman Sayle

ROWMAN AND LITTLEFIELD
Totowa, New Jersey

First published in the United States 1976
by ROWMAN AND LITTLEFIELD, Totowa, N.J.

© Margaret Killip 1976

ISBN 0-87471-771-X

Printed in Great Britain

Foreword

Until the 1830s, when the Liverpool boat service started, the Isle of Man was virtually cut off from the rest of the British Isles. The Editor of *The Manx Advertiser* commented: "Until of late [our country] has been considered as a barbarous coast, scarcely visited save by the adventurer, the treacherous criminal, the smuggler, and the vagabond." The first regular sailings of any sort only date from 1819, when a small-scale service from Whitehaven was established. Forty-five years earlier, the S.P.C.K. reported that, from a population of 20,000, "the greater part speak no English." But in 1874, the Cornishman Jenner found little more than a quarter of the inhabitants who remembered their own language, and only 190 were not bilingual. By this time the tourist industry was under way. It was an interesting phenomenon in its own right, for the Isle of Man was among the very first areas to cater for a working-class clientele. Twenty-seven years later, on the other hand, in 1901, the old speech was only recalled by one in twelve.

Two years before this, Manxmen founded *Yn Cheshaght Ghailckagh* (The Gaelic League) to maintain the language, but now it is confined to enthusiasts and scholars. The island is today known as an attractive holiday centre, with friendly towns, a pretty coastline, and beautiful mountains in the interior. *Farraght yn nyr Barrule* (Built firm as Barrule), says the Manx National Anthem, referring to one of the island's great peaks. This reminds us that Man is an independent constitutional unit within the British Isles, and that late-comers to English-speaking Britain can and do recognise their own distinctive cultural past.

Margaret Killip was born in Man and has lived there all her life. Since 1957, she has worked for the Folklife Survey of the Manx National Museum. A member of a family which has resided in Lonan Parish since records began, she comments: "What you are finding out about is your own background as well as everyone else's." She mentions Thomas Hardy as a special influence, for his novels and poems "contain more of the natural life of the people than any English author I have come across."

From a scholar working in a part of these islands where the Celtic past still thrives, this is a generous acknowledgement. But the debt is mutual. Writing in 1891, Alfred Nutt of *The Folklore Society* stressed the value of Celtic folklore in illuminating our past: "... it is of equal import to the present-day Briton ... the Celt is an abiding element in the imperial life of the British race ... [his] vast body of anonymous and traditional legend ... has at all times faithfully reflected folk-beliefs and folk-aspirations."

Leaving aside the out-dated, imperial reference, Nutt was right. The folk retain from the past whatever coincides with, or can be adapted to, their present inclinations and needs. Though circumscribed by the framework of current social reality, they adapt, create and dispose within the terms of the knowledge with which they are presented, from whatever source. The island's famous three-legged emblem, for example – probably a 13th-century Norman import from Sicily – finds its oldest local interpretation in a coinage inscription of 1668: *Quocunque jeceris stabit* (It will stand wherever you throw it). Christians see it as a symbol of the Trinity, but in the 1940s, because the Nazis liked ancient Teutonic lore, a version appeared as badge of the Belgian *SS.* This accords with those who suppose that it arrived with the Vikings – certainly a possibility, since it resembles an emblem of Thor. The historical background intensifies the study of folk motifs of this kind. But each interpretation has its own value for the folklorist. So does the more commonplace view that the legs represent defiance of the Scots and Irish, and an unwilling subservience to England.

There are still some two million Celtic speakers living in Europe, about half of them in Brittany. The Celts and the inheritors of their culture – and it is time that traditionally Anglophone Britons counted themselves more firmly among them – can no longer afford to express defiance of each other. Trevor Fishlock's articles in *The Times* three years ago, spoke of the Celts making their last stand: "As distinct peoples they have been for 2,000 years a bright thread in the evolution of European civilisation and now they have reached the ultimate crisis in their long march and decline. They are a tough remnant, not a relic, and by the end of the century it will be possible to judge whether they have gouged out for themselves a worthwhile and valid future existence, or have been effectively erased by the progress to which they have contributed much."

Margaret Killip's admirable book is the third in the present series to deal with the Celtic areas of these islands. I very much hope that these volumes will help to ensure that future existence – and that folklore studies will make a valuable contribution of their own.

London University
July 1975

Venetia Newall

Contents

ISLE OF MAN

Point of Ayre

BRIDE

JURBY   ANDREAS

Ramsey Bay

Ballaugh

Sulby   ● **RAMSEY**

BALLAUGH   LEZAYRE   Ballaterson ●
Bishopscourt ●   Maughold Ch ✝

North Barrule ▲   MAUGHOLD

KIRK MICHAEL   Snaefell ▲   ○ Cashtal yn Ard

Manannan's   Neb   The Barony ●
St Patrick's Island   ○ Chair   Beinn y Phott ▲   Abbey
Staarvey ●   Laxey   lands
● **PEEL**   Garraghyn ▲   Chibbyr
GERMAN ▲   Beary   Ballaglass   Pheric
Tynwald Hill   Mountain   Brundal ●   ○ King Orry's Grave
Neb   ○   LONAN   ● **Laxey**
● **St John's**   St Trinian's   Garwick
✝ Church   ONCHAN
PATRICK   Glass ✝ Abbeylands
Dhoo   MAROWN   BRADDAN
Niarbyl ●   ● **Dalby**
Douglas Bay
▲ South Barrule   ● **DOUGLAS**

Lag ny Keeilley ✝   Silverburn   ● Kerrowkeil   SANTON
Cronk ny   MALEW   IRISH
Irree Laa   ARBORY   Rushen
RUSHEN   ■ Abbey   SEA
● **Port Erin**   Castle
● **Port St Mary**   Rushen   Derbyhaven
Cregneash ●   ■ **Castletown**   ✝ St Michael's Island
Spanish Head   Langness
Calf   ○ Sound
of Man

0 1 2 3 4 5
miles

Acknowledgments

Thanks are due to publishers, authors and editors for permission to
refer to or quote from the following books and journals:

E. A. Armstrong, *The Folklore of Birds*, Collins 1958

H. R. Ellis, *The Road to Hel*, Cambridge University Press, 1943

Maire MacNeill, *The Festival of Lughnasa*, Oxford University Press,
1962 (by permission of the Oxford University Press, Oxford)

Lewis Spence, *The Magic Arts in Celtic Britain*, Rider and Co. 1945
Hutchinson Publishing Group Ltd

Sir Hall Caine, *The Deemster*, Chatto and Windus, 1888

Rupert C. Jarvis, *Illicit Trade with the Isle of Man 1671–1765*,
Transactions of the Lancashire and Cheshire Antiquarian
Society, 1945-46

W. W. Gill, *A First, Second* and *Third Manx Scrapbook*, 1929, 1932,
1963, by permission of Lloyds Bank Ltd

J. J. Kneen, *The Place-Names of the Isle of Man*, Yn Cheshaght
Ghailchagh (The Manx Language Society) 1925

David Craine, *Manannan's Isle*, The Manx Museum and National
Trust, 1955

E. M. Megaw, *Manx Fishing Craft*, J. M. M. V.64 1941

W. Cubbon and B. R. S. Megaw, *The Western Isles and the Growth of
the Manx Parliament*, J. M. M. V,66, 1942

B.R.S. Megaw, *The Barony of St Trinian's in Marown*, J. M. M. IV. 62.
1940 *The Barony of Bangor and Sabhal*, J. M. M. IV. 60. 1939 *The
Monastery of St Maughold*, I. O. M. N.H.A. S. Proceedings V. II.
1950

W. Cubbon, *Gleanings from the Books of the Bishop's Barony*, I. O.M. N.
H. A. S. Proceedings. V. II. 1946-50

J. W. Radcliffe, *Place and Field Names of Kirk Bride*, I. O. M. N. H.A.
S. Proceedings, IV. 1940-1942

H. R. Ellis, *The Story of Sigurd in Viking Art*, J.M.M. V. 67. 1942

Introduction

THE ISLE OF MAN might be described as an island that has lacked isolation. Situated in the middle of the Irish Sea, it is too small, only thirty miles by eleven, and too near to its English Scottish and Irish neighbours to have been left unmolested and allowed to develop independently. From earliest times it has lain in the path of migrating peoples and of the spread of cultures, religious ideas and institutions, and has been particularly vulnerable to attack by sea. Its people have lived mostly as crofters, farmers and fishermen, a way of life dating from a remote past. The earliest farmers were the neolithic people who, as herdsmen and corn-growers, set a pattern for living that was to continue through Celtic and Norse times and even into this century, not without change and development, but until mechanization in agriculture came to the Island, and in remote places it came late, old methods and old beliefs and customs lived on side by side.

Archaeologists have discovered something of the daily life of the Celtic people who lived here, and in excavating the sites of Celtic round houses, the homesteads of Celtic chieftains, have provided a material background for the legends of the first centuries AD, detracting a little in the process from the nineteenth-century conception of the style of living of Cuchulain, Conchobar Macnessa and the other famous figures of Celtic romance.

The Manx background, however, is not entirely Celtic; another influence helped to shape our traditions, institutions and national character, that of the Norse rule and culture established here in the ninth century and lasting until the thirteenth. The Vikings brought terror and bloodshed to the Island as they did wherever they went, but as settlers and rulers gave it much: their language, surviving particularly in place-names, their seafaring skill and knowledge, and a form of government that developed out of the Isle of Man's political association with the Hebrides when, after 1079 under Godred Crovan I, they constituted the Kingdom of Man and the Isles, which lasted for nearly two centuries.

In the succeeding period the Isle of Man was little more than a pawn, a spoil of war in the struggle for supremacy between England and Scotland, and as the Manx poet T. E. Brown has said was kicked about like a football. Frequent changes in overlords show this – Piers Gaveston, Edward II's favourite in 1311, Henry de Beaumont in 1312 and previously in 1310, and Thomas Randolph, nephew of Robert Bruce who took the Island in 1313. When finally it fell to the English in 1333, it was sold towards the end of the century to William le Scroop Earl of Wiltshire, and the record of the transaction reveals something of the ambition of these temporary Lords of Man: 'William le Scroop buys of the Lord William de Montacute the isle of Eubonia that is Man. It is forsooth the law of that island that whoever be Lord thereof shall be called King, to whom appertains the right to be crowned with a golden crown.'

More stable government came when in 1406 it was granted by Henry IV to Sir John Stanley, members of whose family as Earls of Derby were first Kings, then Lords of Man. The best remembered in tradition, the seventh Earl, known in the Island as Yn Stanlagh Mooar, The Great Stanley, treated the people with a calculated politeness to gain his own ends: 'a good word, a smile or the like, will cost you nothing,' he wrote to his son, 'but may gain you much.' In 1736 the Isle of Man passed to the related house of Athol, and in 1765 there came the Revestment Act, aimed at putting an end to the smuggling that went on in the Island, whereby it was vested in the British Crown.

The name Isle of Man has given rise to a fair amount of speculation and some witticism, but its connotations are with mountains rather than with men. It was possibly the Norsemen, impressed by its mountainous aspect as they approached it 'west over sea' who bestowed on it the bleak monosyllable *Maun*. Its mountains are not really formidable, only one, Snaefell rising to a height of over 2000 feet. It dominates a central range running from north east to south west, on whose lower slopes clear streams rise among the peat and make their way to the sea through deep tree-shaded glens.

Today, much that is characteristically Manx is disappearing before the onslaught of the ubiquitous developer and moderniser. Some native Manx architecture may still be seen though that too is fast disappearing. The Manx country builder's technique amounted to an up-ending of his environment, and the result could not fail to blend and merge again into the landscape. In the face of ever-encroaching modern development, these old houses and farmsteads, low-built, with small-paned windows and thick walls to keep out the wind, stand out more than ever as the last strongholds of old Manx life. Coming upon them in the shelter of a glen or on a bare hillside fronting the sea, with their quiet reminder of the generations who lived and worked in them, one suspects that more old tales and customs have been told and done and lost and forgotten in and around their walls than assiduous folklorists have ever managed to collect.

With such a continuing threat to these last visible remnants of our recent past, the wisdom and foresight of those who nearly forty years ago were responsible for establishing a Manx Folk Museum, a crofter's house, a small farmstead and craft workshops, in Cregneash in the south of the Island, becomes daily more apparent.

Glossary of Manx-Gaelic and Dialect Words and Place Names

Bons,	Gorse sticks for fuel
Cashtal yn Ard	Castle of the height
Chiallagh	Open hearth
Creg ny Mnuilt	Rock of the wethers
Curragh Glass	Green Marsh
Flaggers	Yellow Iris
Haggart	Stackyard
Jeel	Damage
Mheillea	The cutting of the last sheaf in harvest
Moaney	Turf-ground, here used as a field name
Peck	A skin tray for oatcake
Reaisht	Rough uncultivated ground
Shebeen	An unlicensed ale-house
Street	Farmyard
Unnysup	Corrupt version of the song title 'The hunt is up'
Ugh cha nee	Alas!
Wallad	Bag, pouch

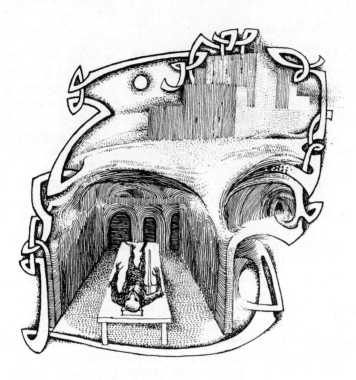

1 The Folk and the Folklorists

FOR FOLKLORISTS IT IS always too late, and for some it was too late even a hundred years ago. A. W. Moore, the Manx historian and folklorist was noting regretfully in 1891:

> The Isle of Man has been unfortunate in not having had competent collectors of its Legendary Lore. But few have taken the slightest interest in it, and those who have did not understand the language in which they could have learned it at first hand ... It is remarkable that no native Manxmen have till recently, troubled themselves about collecting what, we suppose, they considered idle if not mischievous tales ... Now it is unfortunately too late. The Manx language is moribund, and Manx superstitions, except in the more remote districts, are in a similar state.

Looking back to the time when this was being said, it seems now that eighty years ago, life was being lived here in the traditional way, beliefs and customs had scarcely begun to change, and people were still telling the old tales round the chiollagh fire. The writer of this depressing assessment of the state of Manx folklore, himself a man of leisure and a scholar was perhaps expecting too much, certainly of his fellow-countrymen, most of whom were too busy leading the life to make a study of it. His dissatisfaction with the non-Gaelic-speaking strangers who came to the Island and attempted the task of collecting its folklore, and his condemnation of the Manx people who might have collected it and failed to do so, point to difficulties in the task which anyone attempting it would have encountered.

From the amount of material that has come to light since his day, it is obvious that at the time he was writing much of it was still in circulation throughout the Island as a live tradition. This, as far as the stranger was concerned added to the difficulty. Beliefs and customs that still have a hold on people and mean anything to them are locked away in their minds, and not made available to the casual enquiring stranger. Except in rare cases, the native Manxman or woman born into the tradition accepted it, and unless instructed as a few were, our critic among them, by the precept of others, and shown the way, were not capable of taking the necessary detached and objective view of the culture they had inherited. There were notable exceptions, gifted individuals able to stand outside their tradition and observe it. One of them was the lexicographer Archibald Cregeen who foresaw the inevitable fate of Manx Gaelic unless it was recorded, and travelled round the countryside taking down words from the lips of the people in order to compile his Manx dictionary. He saved the language, and in so doing occasionally provided unexpected insights into Manx attitudes – towards labour for instance, as in the leisurely expression 'fer-feayree' – 'one to cool while others are working.'

From a consideration of the methods of the early folklorists it becomes obvious that qualities of personality were as important as scholarly qualifications in laying hold of the coveted knowledge. The Scotsman J. F. Campbell, compiler of *Popular Tales of the West Highlands,* who visited the Island in 1860 in search of similar material here, seems to have fallen short in this respect, for according to A. W. Moore, 'he might have done much for Manx folklore even at such a late period and in spite of his also being a stranger if he had thought it worth his while, but being discouraged at his Gaelic not being understood, and the difficulty of extracting any information from the Manx peasantry, he did not persevere'.

It is remarkable, considering the difficulties that confronted a prospective collector, that the Manx folk and fairy stories ever came to be written down. From time to time however, and almost as if by chance, someone with the right qualities of heart and mind seems to have appeared in our midst, succeeded somehow in penetrating the people's reserve, and was made free of a closely guarded tradition.

The earliest of these, and one of the most copious collectors of Manx folklore, was George Waldron who, while he was in the Island between 1720 and 1730 keeping a watching brief for the British Government and reporting on smuggling activity, noted down many stories from people he met in the course of his duties. He has been criticised as an embellisher of what he heard, an inventor or at least an exaggerator of marvels, which to some extent he no doubt was. But there would certainly have been more widely circulated and far more wonderful tales obtainable in his time, and the contacts he may be assumed to have had among seafaring people generally would have provided him with the best possible sources. There is no doubt that in spite of the criticism levelled at him, he was and is the fountainhead of all our early knowledge of Manx folklore, and the source from which many later writers quote. His credulity, the quality his detractors most derided in him, was an advantage up to a point, allowing him to note down stories which a more cautious observer might, perhaps mistakenly, have dismissed as too improbable. Waldron courageously set all down, though with an occasional disclaimer, a face-saving word of caution.

Manx legends excited his imagination, and by page five of his *Description of the Isle of Man,* he is well launched on a story about Castle Rushen in which there is

> an apartment which has never been opened in the memory of man; the persons belonging to the castle are very cautious in giving any reason for it, but the natives, who are excessively superstitious, assign this: that there is

something of enchantment in it. They tell you that the Castle was at first inhabited by fairies, and afterwards by giants, who continued in the possession of it till the days of Merlin, who by the force of magic dislodged the greatest part of them, and bound the rest in spells, which they believe will be indissoluble to the end of the world ... they say there are a great number of fine apartments underground, exceeding in magnificence any of the upper rooms; several men of more than ordinary courage have in former times ventured down to explore the secrets of this subterranean dwelling-place, but none of them ever returned to give an account of what they saw.

He tells then of a man determined to find out for himself what mysteries underlay the Castle, who having gained permission to go down and provided himself with a clue of packthread to help him find his way back, went down into its depths, travelling by winding passagaes and through dark caverns until he came to a lighted house where a servant led him through the house and set him further on his way.

He then walked a considerable way, and at last beheld another house, more magnificent than the first; and the windows being all open, discovered innumerable lamps burning in every room. Here he designed also to knock, but had the curiosity to step on a little bank which commanded a low parlour; on looking in he beheld a vast table in the middle of the room of black marble, and on it, extended at full length, a man, or rather monster; for by his account, he could not be less than fourteen feet long and ten or eleven round the body. This prodigious fabrick lay as if sleeping, with his head on a book, and a sword by him, of a size answerable to the hand which 'tis supposed made use of it.

The hitherto bold traveller was so terrified by the sight that he decided he had better not 'attempt entrance into a place inhabited by persons of that unequal stature' and set off on his return journey. On his way he met the servant once more and was told that if he had knocked at the second door, he would have seen company enough, but could never have returned.

At this point, with less credulous readers in mind, Waldron makes some pretence of not believing this story himself, but is soon embarked on another even more marvellous. 'Ridiculous as this narrative appears, whoever seems to disbelieve it, is looked on as a person of weak faith; but though this might be sufficient to prove their superstitions, I cannot forbear making mention of another tradition they have, and of a much longer standing.'

Subsequent visitors to the Island who attempted 'to delineate the customs and manners of its inhabitants,' though less concerned with the more extravagant aspects of its folklore, sometimes managed through a chance encounter to learn something about the fairies. David Robertson who came here in 1791 found himself benighted in the mountains, and asked for shelter in a lonely house.

> The sole tenant of this clay-built hut was an aged peasant of a pensive and melancholy aspect. He received me with much hospitality; trimmed his little fire of turf and gorse ... From him I learned that, notwithstanding all the holy sprinklings of the priests of former days, the fairies still haunted many places in the Island: that there were playful and benignant spirits, and those who were sullen and vindictive. The former of these he had often seen on a fine summer evening sitting on the margin of the brooks and waterfalls, or dancing on the tops of the neighbouring mountains. These sportive beings ... rejoiced in the happiness of mortals; but the sullen fairies delighted to procure human misery. These lived apart from others, and were neither beautiful in their persons nor gorgeous in their array. They were generally enveloped in clouds or in the mountain fogs, and haunted the hideous precipices and caverns on the seashore. My host added, that to them Manxsmen imputed all their sufferings.

To the eighteenth-century traveller such tales were merely the imaginings of an ignorant peasantry. This was Robertson's opinion of them, and there were others like him, who listened patiently enough to the people's stories, but afterwards wrote slightingly of them as trifles beneath their notice. Waldron had an appreciation of their value unusual in a man of his time. 'at my first coming to the Island, I was extremely solicitous in diving into the manners and humour of a people which seemed so altogether new, and different from all the other Europeans I had even seen.' Waldron's understanding of our Celtic background seems to have been limited to prejudice against Irish Catholicism, whose priests he reckons were harboured here, while Roman Catholic children were to his horror admitted to the schools, though not to be educated, but to sit in idleness and interest themselves in fables – a significant remark, if only he had said what kind. He like the others spoke often and contemptuously of the people's ignorance and lack of education. He was the typical Englishmen abroad, expecting everyone to speak his language, and oblivious of the fact that he was in a country with its own language and culture. Yet in spite of this he had some sympathy with the people, enough to get many stories from them. If the air of ingenuous enthusiasm reflected from the pages of his *Description of the Isle of Man* is any indication of the kind of man he was, it is possible that, though his approach to Manx folklore was rather random and unscholarly, there were doors opened to him that might have remained closed to a more learned though less genial character.

By the nineteenth century folklorists and scholars of international reputation were beginning to interest themselves in the Isle of Man as part of the Celtic world and its culture. This era of enquiry into our traditions was ushered in by a visit from George Borrow who when he set foot in the Island in 1855 was moved to exclaim: 'A lovelier isle than Vennon G. never saw in his wide career.' To a linguist such as he was the language presented no problems and his interest in it was in fact one of the main reasons for his visit. He travelled about on foot all over the Island into its remotest corners in search of people who could speak it and sing songs in Manx. Of anyone he met on the road he asked, 'Do you speak Manx?; What is the name of the river in Manx? Do you know any Manx songs?' He had one conversation with an old Manxman he met on the quay whose features 'were like those of an ill-tempered Irishman.' 'Have you many witches,' said I, in Man. 'Plenty,' said the old fellow, 'but not so many as formerly; at one time Man was full of witches and wizards ... one of the Kings of Man was a wizard ... he was a giant and had three legs, and they are his legs which you see on the side of the steamer, for those three legs are the arms of Man.' The 'old fellow' seems on the whole to have been treating Borrow to a little of the kind of improvisation on the matter under discussion with which the native population rather later than this learned to amuse themselves at the expense of credulous and enquiring trippers. He went on about the wizard King of Man. 'I believe he was called King Horry ... and he had a wife who knew as much of witchcraft as himself. He called her Ben my Chree, no doubt because he was so fond of her. Well, they are both dead and gone now, but they are not altogether abaft, for two of our best steam packets are called King Horry and Ben my Chree.'

Borrow was greatly interested in Manx folk songs, one in particular of which he often heard from the people he met seems to have captured his fancy, the ballad called *Mylecharane,* which tells of an old miser of that name who found a buried treasure in the Curraghs. The verses are in the form of a question and answer, with a refrain after each line:

O Vylecharane c'raad hooar oo dty stoyr?
My lomarcan daag oo mee,
Nagh dooar mee'sy churragh eh, dowin dowin dy-liooar?
As my lomarcan daag oo mee.
O Mylecharane, where found you your store,
Lonely you did leave me,
Did I not find it deep, deep enough,
And alone you did leave me.

In 1862 Borrow wrote about this song and another *Illiam Dhone (Brown William)* in an article in the periodical Once a Week, in which he tells how during his stay in the Island, his interest in the Mylecharane ballad prompted him to go in search of the place where the Mylecharane family had lived, and if possible find the miser's descendants.

In the autumn of the year 1855 I found my way across the Curragh to the house of John Mollie Charane. On my knocking at the door, it was opened by a respectable-looking elderly female of about sixty who ... asked me to walk in, saying I looked faint and weary. On my entering she made me sit down, brought me a basin of buttermilk to drink, and asked me what brought me to the Curragh. Merely to see Mollie Charane, I replied. Whereupon she said he was not at home, but that she was his wife and any business I had with her husband I might communicate to her. I told her that my only motive in coming was to see a descendant of the person mentioned in the celebrated song. She then looked at me with some surprise, and observed that there was indeed a song about a person of the family, but that he had been dead and gone many a long year, and she wondered I should give myself the trouble to come to such a place as the Curragh to see people merely because one of their forebears was mentioned in a song. I said that however strange the reason I gave might seem to her, it was the true one, whereupon she replied that as I was come I was welcome ... after conversing with the respectable old lady for about half an hour, I got up, shook her by the hand and departed for Balla Giberagh. The house was a neat little white house fronting the west, having a clump of trees near it. However miserly the Mollie Charane of the song may have been, I experienced no lack of hospitality in the house of his descendant.

The book that Borrow intended to write about his visit to the Isle of Man regrettably never was written in any extended form, though he had decided on a title, *Bayr Jiarg as Glion Doo' Red Road and Dark Valley*. Perhaps he found that his stay had been too short, rather less than a fortnight, but in that time he covered most of the Island, and from the notes he made of his wanderings, the people he met and his conversations with them, his impressions of scenes and places, there seems to have been adequate material for a book, especially for a writer of his quality.

Time must have been a limiting factor for anyone coming here and trying to get to know a virtually foreign people, and to understand their way of life and their language. J. F. Campbell cannot be entirely excused on these grounds, nor simply because he did not 'persevere.' He reveals the reason for his lack of success in a first-hand account of his meetings with the people, unconsciously demonstrating how not to go about it. 'The Manxman,' he writes 'would not trust the foreigner with his secrets; his eyes twinkled suspiciously, and his hand seemed unconsciously to grasp his mouth as if to keep all fast.' Someone of his experience should have know that to ask an old person outright 'Will you tell me a story?'

and when nothing was forthcoming to bring moral pressure to bear to get what he wanted, 'What a shame for you, an old Mananach not to tell me a story when I have told you one, and filled your pipe and all!' was not very likely to produce results. The old Manxman on whom he practised these bullying tactics was inclined to be evasive. In reply to Campbell's questions, he spoke of churches in the Island, mentioned the price of tobacco, went so far as to admit that they used to tell *skylls*, tales in the old days, but then excused himself because, he said, he had to go and saw wood.

It was the German Charles Roeder, born in Thuringia, but for long resident in Manchester, and a frequent visitor to the Isle of Man who, perhaps because of some quality the others lacked, succeeded in unearthing the greatest treasure. He had a genuine affection for the Island and its people. 'My love for Ellan Vannin and the Manninee drew me this summer again to the heathery purple hills of the South where the golden gorse and the cushags grow and dream ... I spent some very happy times in the midst of the hospitable and warm-hearted people, and our acquaintance in many instances ripened into intimate friendship.' Roeder met the people on an equal footing as friends, without condescension, a quality they would never tolerate; German 'gemutlichkeit' seems to have won them over, where Celtic charm and scholarship failed or only partially succeeded, and he was asked into their homes and given a seat by the chiollagh. 'Many were the long summer noons we sat together at the turf fire, talking and laughing and feasting in true Manx style.' He treated the material he gathered and the givers of it with equal respect: 'I have put myself in the background and prefer to let my friends act and talk ... I have not mended or clipped and this their speech runs and tinkles on in a channel I was fain to fix and preserve and show the national pulse. There you have the fragrance and gossamer that floats in the country.'

During his visits Roeder stayed with the family of Edward Faragher of Cregneash, who was a local poet, a writer of verse in Manx and English, and better known by his nickname Ned Beg Hom Ruy. He had a great fund of local knowledge and Manx lore in general which Roeder gently extracted from him, and after he left the Island corresponded with him for a number of years. Their letters show mutual liking and respect, although now and then a faint note of exasperation is heard in

Edward Faragher's replies when Roeder, pursuing his search for fairy lore with Teutonic thoroughness, poses a more than usually preposterous enquiry, 'I do assure you,' he writes in one letter, acknowledging some books and a gift of tobacco from Roeder, 'I know very little about talking birds and singing water and little green dogs with one ear.'

These searchers after Manx tradition, and their successors who followed their example in the early years of this century, became increasingly aware of its academic value as the years passed. They no longer listened to the tales in amazement like Waldron, they grew more like Campbell and knew what they wanted to hear. Their interest was in the fairly tale, the old Celtic or Norse legend not the tellers of them, in the song, not the singer. There is no doubt that they missed a good deal; all the ground was not covered as Roeder covered the south, but they rescued a vast quantity of folklore from the oblivion that would certainly have overtaken it without their efforts. Even if as they worked some were mainly concerned with their personal contribution to scholarship and they milked the Manx people relentlessly of their oral traditions to further their own ends, we have every reason to be grateful to them, since they gave it back to us again in written form.

Its importance will probably increase, not diminish, because there is now and seems to have been for some time a gradual dispersal of the Manx people. The young are leaving the Island, old names and families are dying out. We are no longer as in the days of emigration in danger of becoming 'lost in the Empire's mass': the traffic is now rather the other way, and with the final disintegration of the Empire the Manx remnant in the Island is becoming outnumbered by a steady influx of strangers, from various parts of the world, many from former Commonwealth countries, but whatever their origin, with one thing in common, the possession of apparently unlimited wealth, with which to buy up the land.

The disappearance of a minority, its way of life, traditions and spiritual outlook can pass almost unnoticed, and only those who constitute it are conscious of what is happening and what is being lost. There is added sadness in this trend towards national extinction in the realization that the Manx people have never been adequately written about, though many have attempted it. They have been caricatured, defamed, sentimentalized and romanticized, but no writer has emerged capable of interpreting the people of the Island to themselves. Some may say T. E. Brown has done it, and presumably recognise themselves, in Betsy Lee, Tommy Big-Eyes, and the rest of his characters.

Those who cannot do this, have the record of the folklorists and the insight they provide into the life of the Island and its people. To compensate for the lack of a convincing fictional portrayal, there are the fictions of the collective Manx mind drawn from the people themselves, and a true reflection of their life and background.

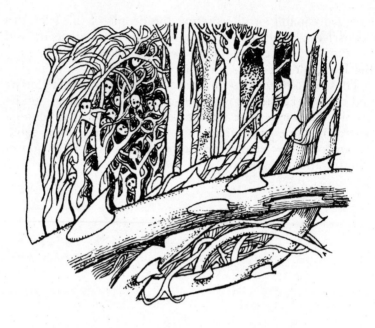

2 The Fairy Belief

TO WRITE ABOUT fairy beliefs at all is difficult, almost presumptuous, since it is an attempt to enter and find one's way about in a country that is only knowable to those who are born into it and so inherit it by natural right. Most Manx people whose elders' recollections reach back to the beginning of this century or even further, can still claim to have a small share in it, and are able to lay hold of a few fragments of what they heard of it in childhood. Vague memories of the *buggane* that used to haunt a lonely road, and was heard roaring on the hill by someone going home late at night, and about the fynnoderee, a strange creature, neither fairy nor human being, living away up in the mountains but coming down to the farms to work secretly by night, who refused to wear the suit of clothes a farmer left for him. Best remembered of all, stories of the fairies dressed in red caps and green coats living among the nut trees down by the river. Everyone knew how they used to waylay people when they were coming home late, along a dark road or across a field, and so bewilder them that they lost all sense of direction and wandered about until morning unable to find their way.

It is likely enough that tales of this kind could still be heard if in this disbelieving age people dared to tell them. They cannot all be forgotten. Thirty or so years ago they were being told quite as a matter of course, especially in a gathering of country people by those who did not so much consciously believe them, as having heard them all their days from parents and grandparents, found acceptance of them a natural habit of mind. To say that the tellers of the tales didn't believe them is not true; they probably more than half believed them. It was not uncommon to hear a personal experience of being waylaid by the fairies being told very convincingly by a man who remembered wandering with confused mind round his own field all night until daylight came, unable to find a gate he was in the habit of opening every day of his life.

The sensation of being 'took' by the fairies is not unheard of even today. Superstitions believed to have been entirely banished lie dormant in the minds of those who once knew them, and a sudden fright or strange happening will bring them to the surface though they may not have been thought of for years. Not many people have really seen a ghost or a buggane, but a good many have momentarily thought they had, though the ghostly figure turned out in the end to be a white sheet drying on the hedge, and the huge bulk of the buggane looming ahead in the dark nothing more than an over-grown clump of gorse.

The black-out of the last war provided conditions comparable to those people must have been all too familiar with in the past, when once night fell, the darkness was total and unrelieved. Travelling uphill, the sky gave some faint illumination, but going down was like walking about at the bottom of a well. In these favourable conditions of the 1940s the fairies recovered powers lost to them for years. Just how many were 'took' by them on those dark nights of the war is not on record, but one woman returning home after dark and deciding to take a short cut across a gorse-grown 'moaney' instead of keeping to the road, lost her bearings and wandered around all night hopelessly astray. She was a woman belonging to a generation familiar with the taking power of the fairies, and probably knew of people who had experienced it, and in the confusion and desperation that grew on her as she wandered blindly through gorse and briar, she finally lost her hold on reality and succumbed to the old persuasive powers. Speaking of it afterwards she said that now and then she would see a light for a moment in the distance, and would try to reach it, but all the time she could feel the fairies 'drawing her away'. It was something that could have happened to anyone with her background, the old inborn fears taking possession of the mind when it was weak and confused.

The belief in being taken by the fairies was so prevalent in the Island that it can scarcely have died out even yet given the right circumstances. It was not only older people who were affected by it, it was being passed on to children. One night some years ago a little boy of eight or nine years old came to the door of a farmhouse crying and saying he was afraid to go home. He lived about a mile further on and the rest of his way was along a lonely road overshadowed and darkened by trees, but when he was asked what he was afraid of, he didn't give the expected answer, that he was frightened of the dark, but 'I'm afraid I'll be took'. The possibility of being made away with or at least of being made sport of by the fairies was always there, and may be still. It's not so very long since people would make a joke of it, and when they were taking leave of each other and saying goodnight, would add as an afterthought 'And mind you won't be took!'

To come across someone today who still retains their inherited knowledge of the fairy world is a strange experience. He or she is not a mere teller of stories, though there have been and still are a good many of these in the island, for fairy tradition reaches a stage when it merely becomes part of the repertoire of story-tellers, raconteurs of some local repute, for whom what they relate no longer has any real meaning. The true believers, if they can be called that, for they are never consciously so, require no audience and in fact possess knowledge they may never tell to anyone. They are far more likely to keep it hidden, but if inadvertently they let slip a hint of familiarity with a supernatural dimension, the person listening experiences a strange sensation, as if a glimpse had been given of a country heard of but hitherto unrealised, or even seriously conceived of. It's one thing to read about fairyland, it's quite another to be shown into it.

There are some people still to be found to whom the fairy

world has some kind of reality, though their numbers are diminishing almost daily. They are the successors, and retain the peculiar visionary insight of those former generations to whom the whole Island was a fairy land, who knew or had heard, had even seen creatures not of this world inhabiting every acre of it. There was hardly a glen or hill or farm that was not their haunt, a place where something was 'taking', from more familiar spirits like the fairies themselves, black dogs and bugganes lurking among human habitations, to stranger things roaming at large in wilder places and only to be met with occasionally, a white unicorn that appeared on the mountains, a phantom wolf heard howling among them, the *purr mooar*, an equally spectral pig, and the *goayr heddagh*, a ghostly goat, to make a random selection.

For the uninitiated even to realise its existence, let alone enter and inhabit this vanished country of the mind, requires a considerable effort of imagination, and where it exists, at least a temporary suspension of disbelief; also humility and an unsophisticated eye. Right attitudes were always important in fairy dealings. There is a story about a little hunchback shoemaker, Tom Beg, who met a very splendid company of fairies among the mountains, and was rewarded by having his hump removed because he was polite and courteous to them, and only counted the days of the week up to Saturday; but his brother Bill Beg was rude to them, and so ignorant of what was acceptable to them that he actually mentioned Sunday in their hearing, so that as a punishment, another hump was added to the one he had already.

Perhaps one reason why J. F. Campbell failed to get the stories he wanted from the people was that he failed to realize their value to those who knew them. He was flippant about what were to them matters of serious belief. Scholars and folklorists tend to regard the old beliefs objectively and in order to classify and categorize them and make some kind of order out of chaos, take them out of the people's minds where they properly belong. For the fairies have no existence for us apart from the people who believed in them and met them as they went about their work, and who as they travelled along the roads never lacked for company.

The fairy belief was a creed as real as any to those who professed it. It did not merely underlie a more orthodox religious faith, but existed alongside it. A woman who said, 'I heard most of the fairy stories I know from an old man who used to teach me in Sunday School', was stating a fact. The old faith for many people had an earlier though not necessarily a prior claim, and up to a certain point in time, sooner for some than others, it could never be said that Christian teaching had succeeded in banishing a belief in fairies from their minds. It was used sometimes as a weapon against them. If someone met a company of fairies on the road, and as often happened they crowded and obstructed the way, they could most effectively be dispersed by repeating a line from a hymn 'Jesus the Name high over all, In Heaven or Earth or Sky', but there was no doubt in the mind of the person piously making this invocation that the fairies were there.

The effect on each other of Christian and fairy belief, and the distinctions made by fairies and other creatures between churches and denominations might repay investigation. The Catholic Church they recognized as a worthy opponent: it was a pre-Reformation church that was haunted by an evil spirit in the form of a buggane, and it was a Roman Catholic priest who could put rest on a troubling spirit, and banish an evil one, usually to the Red Sea. But when the fairies encountered the Protestants, especially the Methodists there seemed to be no fight left in them, they just went away. A company of them that had always lived in Glen Drink, had been there for so long that they had even given it its name, Glen of the Dancing, were never seen there again after a Primitive Methodist chapel had been built nearby. These particular fairies it seems, 'objected to dissent'.

The existence in the Isle of Man of apparently conflicting religious faiths was nothing new. Its peoples had probably known them from earliest times, and had plenty of practice in broadening their outlook to accommodate the new notions and new gods brought to them by many invaders. Though a conservative nation by nature, it is unlikely that we readily relinquished the old in favour of the new. It was perhaps the challenge of frequent change that gave rise to a much-quoted Manx proverb, *Mannagh vow cliaghtey cliaghtey nee cliaghtey coe.* 'If custom beget not custom, custom will weep'. It was our habit to keep what we had, and absorb something of the new. Odin of the Norsemen never usurped the place of Manannan, but there are traces of him in Manx folklore, and Norse stories found a new setting among the Manx glens.

This long cultivated habit of tolerance to new ideas might account for the ease with which it was possible to reconcile a belief in fairies with a belief in God. Many people probably managed to live quite comfortably in both worlds, and personal instances of this are not lacking. There was one man and rather surprisingly a Methodist, about whom there always hung the uncanny aura of someone who was known to have dealings with the fairies. People were not exactly afraid of him, but eyed him speculatively, wondering just how much he knew, and if he really went where he was said to go. He was supposed to be able to summon the fairies whenever he wanted them, in his own house, which wasn't all that remarkable if he really had the power, as he lived half-way up a mountain-side near to fairy haunts. One Sunday night a friend of his who lived over the hill in the next parish, came to his house for supper after chapel. It was a summer evening, but it was getting late, and once supper was over, time for a traveller to be getting on his way. People often felt uneasy in that house once the sun had gone down behind the mountain. There was a cupboard in the corner behind the old man's armchair, and though nobody had ever seen it opened, it was believed that it was there he went to call the fairies to do his bidding. He got up from his seat to see the visitor to the door, and then suggested that as he had a middling lonely road to go, maybe he would like a bit of company on the way, and turned to the cupboard in the corner. His friend refused the offer very firmly and hurried out through the door and up the hill towards Gob ny Geay, and all the way home kept looking behind him, dreading to see the kind of 'company' that might be following him.

This Wesleyan with a cupboard as anteroom to a private fairy world was doubtless an exception, and Methodism has to be given the credit – or blame – for wooing the people away from superstition. Under the aegis of the Church the old faith seemed to survive, even to flourish, but there was something about Methodism, that blighted it. The fairies apparently knew when they had met their match, and it was made clear to them that they could never hope to be among the elect. One of them met a travelling Wesleyan preacher one night crossing the mountains and asked him who should be saved. 'Only those who are of flesh and blood', replied the preacher sternly, and the fairy went away wailing, *'Cha vel ayrn erbee aym ayns Chreest'* 'I have no share in Christ'.

Roeder's phrase for the fairy tradition, 'the gossamer that floats in the country', conveys its nature exactly. It was everywhere yet almost invisible, seemed always on the point of vanishing, but still to be found clinging around every house and tree and field and glen. The fairies themselves were just as evanescent as the stories about them, and scarcely ever to be thought of as creatures of flesh and blood.

> There was a woman who once intercepted the fairies when they attempted to carry off two girls who fell asleep one night outside the door of the house when they were waiting for a sow to farrow, and was carried off herself in the struggle with them. Next morning a large pool of blood was found outside the door. The fairies had tried to steal the sleeping girls but the person who had been carried off by them prevented it: this so angered the fairies that they killed her. It could not have been a fairy that was killed, as they have no blood.

A fairy changeling would neither eat nor drink and seemed to lie all day in its cradle without moving, though it could get up and dance when it had a mind to. It was because of its strange non-human behaviour and its failure to thrive and grow as a normal child should, that its other-world nature was suspected.

Besides being immaterial bodily, the Manx fairies seem to have been nameless. By what name they were known to Gaelic speakers before the word 'fairy' came into use is something of a mystery. In the fairy stories collected, or at least in those written down over the last seventy or eighty years, they are often spoken of as 'themselves': 'One of Themselves told me to come to London Bridge and I would find a fortune' or 'After a moment of uproar Themselves missed the cup'. The Manx-Gaelic equivalent of this, 'ad-hene' as a name for them, seems to be entirely absent from any dictionary or glossary of old forgotten words, though there are other Manx-Gaelic fairy names on record *Ny Mooinjer Veggey* (The Little Kindred), *Ny Guillyn Beggey* (The Little Boys), *Yn Sleih Veggey* (The Little People), all terms that are commonly used in English when speaking of the fairies, but the Gaelic *ad-hene,* though possibly a quite genuine orally-transmitted name, never seems to have appeared in its original Gaelic form. There is justification for it in the substitution in everyday speech of 'himself', and 'herself' for someone's name, once a very common idiom in the Isle of Man. *Vel eh-hene ec y thie?* (Is himself at home?) *'C'raad t'ee hene?'* ('Where's herself?'); but it doesn't seem to have been used in the plural, and 'themselves' is an expression that is absent from the stories taken down by word of mouth by people like Roeder; which encourages one to entertain the unworthy suspicion that it was a name that took the fancy of late nineteenth century re-tellers of fairy stories.

Apart from these designations and a few others 'the crowd' and 'the mob beg', the fairy clan were curiously anonymous in the Isle of Man. Though spoken of now generally as the fairies, the word is an English importation, probably a reasonably early one, introduced that is 'more than a hundred years ago', and long enough in circulation to have acquired a Gaelic form *ferrish* which occurs in a number of place-names as also does 'fairy' – *Close ny Ferrishyn, Chibbyr ny Ferrishyn;* Fairy Hill and Fairy Cottage, the two latter still well known.

A much older name for them, though its spoken use is no longer remembered is *ny Shee,* the same word as the Irish *Sidh.* It is to be recognized in the name of the Lhiannan Shee, the Woman of the Fairies, and must once have been a name given to those who lived in green mounds and hills which go by names like Cronk ny Shee, the Hill of the Shee, Glion ny Shee and Purt-e-Chee, the Glen and possibly, the Fort of the Shee respectively.

In dialect they were often spoken of as 'ones' or as 'them'. There can be no doubt that all these names arose from the necessity to address them and refer to them obliquely rather than directly. With the fairies and all other supernatural beings, it was unwise to call them by their known name, to speak of them openly as fairies, and the converse also was true; to reply when they called a human being by name was to be delivered into their power. There is a dialect poem that tells of a farmer's daughter who heard her name being called when she was out in the fields, and who answered it:

> I was down alone in the Moaney,
> Nobody else was near,
> When my name was goin' a' callin'

Low an' sof' an' clear;
None was I seein' aroun' me
Never a face of clay,
An' my name was goin' a' callin'
Jus' at the close of day.

Her mother tells her that it is only the children calling her to come and play, or her father wanting her to help him to drive the sheep, but the girl replies –

There's Them that's sometimes callin'
Low in the evenin' hour
And if you give them answer
They have you in their power;

and her mother realises then that she is beyond human help –

What ails thee, chile veen, what ails thee?
I answered it, she said.

The power of the name, of calling or even knowing a person's name is a common theme in folk tales. Rumpelstiltskin comes to mind as one of the best-known examples, and a Manx story of this kind, *The Lazy Wife,* tells of a woman who is too lazy to spin the rolls of wool her husband brings her, and is helped by a giant who agrees to do the spinning for her provided she can guess his name by the time the work is done, and she comes to get the thread. When the time is up, she goes to his house, and though she has found out his name, she makes a few wrong guesses just to make him suppose she doesn't know it, but at last she comes out with it: 'Mollyndroat', a name which proves her helper to have been no common giant if it means what it seems to mean 'servant of the druid'. She has fulfilled the conditions and found out his name, so the giant in spite of his magicianly lineage, can do her no harm, and has to let her have the thread.

Whatever the ambiguity of the names the fairies were known by, they are all of a collective kind, and prove them to have been gregarious by nature, and they were almost invariably met with in hosts or armies, as troops of horsemen and hunters, in groups large or small, rarely singly or as solitary wanderers. There were other supernatural creatures, not to be numbered among 'the mob beg', who lived a solitary existence, appeared alone, and each had a distinctive name, the *fynnoderee, lhiannan shee, buggane* and *glashtin*. They belonged to a different breed from the Little People, and were usually of human and sometimes of superhuman strength and stature. The fairies themselves were not of uniform small size, though some were very diminutive, only inches high; others like children 'as big as little seven-year old boys' and a few were seen who appeared to be of near-human height. They were not noticeably beautiful, but inclined to have pale faces and rather small eyes, and their ears too were small in proportion. Once when two men were driving their cows home in the evening, they saw a little man five or six inches high walking along the road before the cows' feet:

> he was very small and had no beard and a little pale face and his ears were only as big as a shirt button. He was dressed in blue, and could walk as fast as the cows ... but when they were just going to lay hold of him, he spread the wings of his little coat, and rose up to the clouds and was out of sight in a minute. He had very little feet and shoes, and left no footprints on the dust of the road.

These small fairies, both men and women, were nimble and agile, could jump and leap about and were great dancers. They were particularly fond of doing what the old-style folklorists described as 'sporting in the trees'; they would gather together in the glen and passers-by would hear them in the trees making a lot of noise and chattering in some unintelligible tongue. They liked most of all to swing and play in the elder trees, and these were always thought of as fairy trees in the Isle of Man. There wasn't a house or farm that didn't have its 'tramman' tree planted by the door or in the garden 'for the fairies'. Many of them are still to be seen; the single tree will have grown into a thicket, hiding the old ruined house, but a sure sign that a house once stood there. Hall Caine knew this very well, and describes an old house:

> The door lintel had gone, and the sill of the window had fallen off. There was a round patch of long grass where the well had been, and near to where the porch once stood, the tramman tree still grew ... and though the good people who

had lived and died there were gone from it for ever, the sign
of their faith ... lived after them.

When the wind was blowing the branches, it was then that the
fairies were believed to be riding in the tramman trees, but it
was said that they would desert a house or farm where the
trees had been cut down. This must have happened only very
rarely: no-one would cut a branch of the tramman, let alone
the tree itself, but if it was done, the fairies grieved. 'The old
trammans at Ballakoig were cut down, and the fairies came
every night to weep and lament.'

Not all the fairies went about the world bewailing their lost
hope of salvation and mourning for lost places. They were met
with in all kinds of companies and sometimes in very martial
mood, drilling and marching and giving passwords like the
fairy army encountered by the hunchback cobblers. It could
be hazardous to meet with these fairy warriors, as you were
liable to become involved in the battle. A woman going over
North Barrule one night was unfortunate enough to come
across two armies preparing to fight; they were only waiting
for the sound of a bell to give them the signal to advance, and
as she came level with them, the bell was rung and they set on
each other and in the mêlee she was at once taken prisoner.

Their fighting was sometimes only play, and though they
had a reputation for being reluctant to cross water, there was
a Santon man who said he once 'saw the little people havin' a
thremenjus water fight in the Santon burn up by
Ballaglonney, splashin' and shoutin' and kickin' the water all
over each other, the li'l scuts.' There was once another kind of
fight at Ballaglonney bridge, when some Irish fairies came
over and fought the Manx fairies there, and the prisoners they
took, they put to death by hanging them in the trees.

People were afraid when they heard the fairy huntsmen
riding at night. In Kirk Rushen they used to be heard, a lot of
riders hunting on the mountain at the Howe, with their dogs
yowling and their whips cracking. The wild hunters they were
calling them, and anyone who was in their path was in danger
of his life. A man coming home late one night was overtaken
by some fairy hunters: 'the road was not what it is now, but
very narrow and bad . . . and there was such a terrible
thundering noise and cracking of whips and barking of dogs,
and the whole host passing'. He hadn't a chance to get over

the hedge, but he hid in a doorway until they had gone by.

It is astonishing with what ease and how casually the most ordinary mortals gained entry to fairy land. There were once two farm workers who had been ploughing all day in some stony fields, and although it was Holy Eve and work should have been finished, their plough bars were so bent and crooked by the end of the day that they had to go to the smithy to have them straightened. As they were coming back with the irons over their shoulders, they came to a house with light streaming from the windows and the sound of music coming from inside. They looked in through the windows and saw a great gathering of people and beautiful ladies dancing, so they went and knocked at the door and were invited in. One of them went at once and joined in the dancing and when his turn came drank from the cup of wine that was going round. The other only stood and watched and refused the cup when it was offered to him, and after a while he went home and left his companion behind, and saw nothing more of him for a twelvemonth. The next Holy Eve he thought he would go again to the fairy house and see if he could find out what had become of him. When he came to the house, he knocked and was asked in as before and found his friend just as he had left him, dancing with the fairies and the plough irons over his shoulder. This time he caught him by the arm to draw him out of the dance, and he came quite willingly, and went home with him, thinking he had been away no more than a day.

The people of the Island have always had a well-tuned ear, ever alert to a fine tune. It might be an exaggeration to say that they could pluck one out of the air, but they could certainly hear it in water. Some of the fiddle and clarinet players who accompanied the singing in church and chapel were fond of trying to pick up tunes in strange out of the way places. They would sit by a stream and listen to the sound of it flowing, then try to find the notes they heard and shape the tune on their fiddles. Fairy music they found particularly compelling, and when fairy fiddlers tuned up and started to play, even old men had to dance.

Music was one of the fairies' several devices for luring people away. Sometimes they carried them off by force or called them away by name; or they resorted to crafty methods like enticing a hungry traveller with the sound of sharpening knives and chopping up of meat as if in preparation for a feast, but the playing of music was one of their more subtle allurements.

It was music that drew Donagher Lowey, a farmer of Kirk Rushen into the Fairy Hill, where he would have stayed for ever, if he hadn't had the presence of mind to pour away the wine he was offered instead of drinking it. A man swimming his horse across Douglas river in flood heard a burst of music that brought horse and man to a standstill, and kept them motionless in midstream for nearly half an hour; and a young sailor travelling home over the mountains was so bewitched by the sound of the fairies' hunting horn when the fairy host rode by, that he almost went after them. He thought it 'the finest horn in the world', but if he had followed it he would have been a lost man.

Of all the fairy music that assailed the ears of Manx mortals, the most tantalising and elusive was 'the fairy tune'. Manx fiddlers were always in great demand, and often had to go long distances to play at weddings, mheilleas and similar occasions, for no gathering was complete without them. Sometimes on their way they would chance to hear in some lonely place, a strain of music which they recognised immediately as the fairy tune. What made it most tantalising to the fiddler who heard it was that although it was the most beautiful music in the world, so that he had to stay and listen until he knew it by heart, he always found that after a while, the tune slipped from his mind and when he got home it had gone entirely as if he had never heard it.

There was only one man who ever claimed that he got the fairy tune and never lost it again, and that was old Bill Pheric.

Bill Pheric was coming home late one night across the mountains from Druidale, and heard the fairies singing, just as he was going over the river by the thorntree that grows there. The tune they had was *Bollan Vane,* and he wanted to learn it from them, so he went back three times before he could pick it up and remember it, but after the third time he had it by heart. Just then the sun got up and the fairies went away, for they always go at sunrise. He came home whistling the tune, and since then it has been popular and much played on the fiddle. Many people think that Bill Pheric invented the tune, but he didn't, he got it from the fairies.

With such tenuous and dissolving strains in their keeping, it is no wonder that the fairies preferred the quiet places of the Island: as the world became more noisy they fled in search of solitude and silence. They never tried to avoid human beings, only the noise and disturbance of their new inventions, from iron ploughs to water mills. Where they went and what became of them, or whether they are still here no-one knows for certain, though there are many rumours of their being driven from their old haunts and reports of their going.

Some met a cruel end. A farmer in Jurby so begrudged the expense of providing supper for them every night, and the broken crockery and havoc in the kitchen if the food was forgotten, that he waited up one night for them, and while they were eating and drinking, grabbed them up in handfuls and shut them down in a barrel and threw them in the sea.

There were others strange to say who seem to have put to sea of their own accord. A party of them were seen going out off Laxey beach, and one of the last places where they were seen in the north of the Island was at Lough Goayr in Kirk Bride, one summer evening at dusk, cracking their whips and shouting *'Hoi, son N'herin!'* ('Hey, for Ireland!').

All this seagoing was very uncharacteristic behaviour for beings who, though they would carry a benighted traveller over fields and hedges to the brink of the cliff would not step over the edge. 'Religion' has been blamed for their disappearance: 'Me mother used to say there was more fairies in when she was young before there were so many churches and chapels in; it was the churches and chapels drove them out'.

They seemed to desert a place when they sensed that the old order of things they had known was passing away. They were intolerant of anything new or strange and not at all adaptable: all had to be as it had been. They could stand noise provided it was of their own making, and over the years had become accustomed to the whirr of the spinning wheel and the clatter of the loom: sometimes they did a bit of spinning themselves, but when people started to build mills for working the wool and the cloth, the noise of it was too much for them and they went away.

The fairies who lived in the valley below Beary mountain were seen one rainy day climbing the mountainside and disappearing in the mist, driven away by the noise of a tuck

mill that had been built on the river in the glen below, a place
that had been their home for hundreds of years. Wherever
they were going, they went as fugitives, carrying with them
their worldly or other-worldly goods, and in no account of the
fairies' disappearance do they seem more pathetic or more like
human beings. The person who saw them go heard early one
Spring morning

> floating on the air a low murmuring wailing noise. When
> going to the door to see what occasioned it, behold there
> were multitudes of the 'good people' passing over the
> stepping stones in the river, and wending their way up the
> side of the hill until they were lost in the mist that then
> enveloped the top of Beary mountain. They were chiefly
> dressed in Loaghtan [Manx wool] with little pointed caps,
> and most of them were employed in bearing on their
> shoulders various articles of domestic use, such as kettles,
> pots and pans, the spinning wheel and such-like . . .
> evidently seeking fresh and more quiet quarters, having
> been disturbed, it is supposed, by the noise of a fulling mill
> lately erected in their neighbourhood.

3 Witchcraft: Art-Magic

WITCHCRAFT, LIKE SOME OTHER phenomena that reached the Island across the Irish sea and became separated from its origins, tended to follow its own course and deviated to some extent from the norm, if in the crazed world of witchcraft any standard of normality can be said to exist.

In the opinion of some folklorists its divergence from the more widely known and highly publicised forms of the witch cult, with their covens and witches sabbaths, stems from the early form of Druidism in which it was rooted. 'Witches in Gaelic-speaking lands resembled their compatriots and confreres the Gaelic druids in working single-handed and in a comparatively small way.' The Manx witch was as malevolent and as full of evil intent to 'blight, blast, stunt, wither and destroy' as members of the sisterhood elsewhere, but the evidence that her powers were reinforced by attendance at ceremonial witch assemblies, or that she submitted herself to any organised ritual or had personal dealings with the devil, though not entirely absent, is slight and very localised.

The Manx witch male or female, the charmer, the wise man and woman, worked their spells and charms, both good and bad, murmured their incantations and prepared their potions alone and in secret, unassisted by human and as far as is known any other agency. They were individual performers, and their powers were such that they could if necessary cure from a distance, so that a sick animal or person would begin to show signs of recovery before the person consulting the charmer reached home.

The charmers have been compared to the druids, but any attempt to find a druidical derivation for their skills and methods of working would be unnecessarily ambitious. A Manx practitioner of the magic art has no need to search for an ancestry; he had an early prototype in the legendary first ruler of Man, Manannan Mac Lir, 'a celebrated merchant who was in the Isle of Man ... he understood the dangerous parts of harbours, and from his prescience of the change of the weather always avoided tempests'. His name means Manannan Son of the Sea, and the sea was his natural element over which he had such mastery that when he crossed it, 'For the space of nine waves he would be submerged in the sea, but would rise on the crest of the tenth without wetting chest or breast'. Manx fishermen it is said used to invoke his name when putting to sea, as their natural protector and guardian, until St Patrick took over his role:

> *Manannan Beg Mac y Leirr*
> Little Manannan Son of the Sea,
> Who blessed our Island,
> Bless us and our boat,
> Going out well, coming in better,
> With living and dead in our boat.

Manannan is still well-remembered in the Isle of Man, where, in spite of his sea-roving nature, he lived in a castle on top of Barrule. He is reputed to be buried here also, his grave, one of the more notable of the many giants' graves, a grassy mound by the sea below the walls of Peel Castle. The Island provided him too with a vantage point from which he might survey his kingdom, Manannan's Chair, an earthwork alongside the Staarvey Road in the windy uplands of Kirk German. He used his powers of necromancy to defend the land, and 'by art-magic' could make one man standing on a headland appear like a hundred, and a few chips of wood flung into the water increase to a mighty fleet. He had lost none of this skill by the time the Vikings came, and when he saw them sailing into Peel Bay 'he made little boats of the flaggers by the river side, a good number of them, and put them in the stream. Now when the little fleet came out of the harbour, he caused them to appear like great ships of war, and the enemies' fleet on the bay were in a great panic, and hoisted sails as fast as possible and cut their cables, and got away from the Island.'

With such a founder and ruler the Isle of Man early acquired a reputation as a seat of magic, which it has kept ever since. Manannan was in himself equal to a whole host of druids and travelled all over the Celtic world in many forms and disguises. He had, among other things at his command, a swift horse Enbarr that could travel over land and sea, impregnable armour, and a death-dealing sword called the Answerer; a fairy branch 'with nine apples of red gold upon it' whose music when it was shaken would bring 'forgetfulness of sorrow and woe'.

He had moreover a cloak of invisibility familiar to his island people to this day. Long ago, mariners sailing the Irish sea caught occasional glimpses of the Island through the mists that drifted round it, and came to regard it as a place that seemed almost perpetually hidden, as if defended by enchantment. They were not wrong in their surmise, for when his kingdom was threatened with invasion or any kind of danger Manannan used his art-magic to raise mists that enveloped it and hid it from view, a habit that Manx people believe he has not quite relinquished, for there are times when he still seems to exercise this power. Not many years ago, for the precise period of a royal visit, three days and no longer, the Island was completely concealed in a blanket of mist that stretched from the Calf to the Point of Ayre. The significance of this could not be disregarded, and people looked knowingly at each other and murmured slyly and rather gleefully about 'Manannan's cloak'.

In Manx tradition Manannan appears with rather diminished stature as a purely local ruler to whom his people brought a tribute of green sedge each midsummer; he was known also as a skilled navigator and a tricky magician, seen in the form of a three-legged man rolling down cliffs and issuing out of hills, a tradition about him that the Isle of Man shares with the county of Leinster, but he never stands out as the mysterious and powerful figure Irish mythology proves him to have been; his influence as one of the chief gods of the Celtic world, and the Lord of its Otherworld, extending far beyond the confines of his little island. Our conception of him may be nearer the truth – the first man who ever held Man, as the Manx Traditional Ballad plainly describes him – but there has to be taken into account his larger appearance in the Irish Literature, which has made a god of him, and created out of the events of his life and of those of his peers a mythology in which the Island takes its place. It was Manannan's Isle, and in the geography of the Celtic world was sometimes thought of, as were some other islands, as the Land of Promise, the Island in the Western Sea, to which Manannan himself conducted the fortunate immortals.

It is possible that Manannan may be a composite personality representing a whole dynasty of Celtic rulers, and that the art-magic ascribed to him concentrates in one person the supernatural practices and beliefs of an entire people. The surviving knowledge of magic and witchcraft, much of which has been kept alive and passed on by word of mouth, no doubt derives from many sources, more recent as well as ancient, but some of it appears to be a residue of the wisdom, the medical knowledge, divinatory method and religious ritual of unspecified earlier times, not necessarily or solely from the 'time of the druids' or from the celtic era.

Celtic heroes presumably died like everyone else, but the Celtic mind rejected the concept of death, and seems never to have reconciled itself to a mortal fate. Its conception of the after-life was an extension of present existence in a land of immortal beings, a state to which the more fortunate attained, somehow by-passing the decay and dissolution of death in the Celtic Elysium where no-one grew old or died, and physical power and beauty increased.

The Island must once have lain very near the heart of that romantic ambience with which the poets invested the Celtic west. Even yet in some of its less ravaged places, the old glamour can still be sensed as when it was perhaps –

Eamhain of the apples, Eamhain the delightful,

The Rath to which fair art is welcome ...
The smooth-plained Manaan ...

But though a good deal of this Celtic background underlies
and undoubtedly has influenced Manx supernatural tradition
and ritual, it is possible that the Celtic derivation has
sometimes been over-emphasised, as the Norse was to be later,
and certain alien strains can be separated out, one in
particular that seems quite at variance with the world of Celtic
magic and immortality, a preoccupation with death and the
grave which must surely derive from another age and another
culture, even further back than Celtic times.

It seems strange that the descendants of a race who once
believed in the deathless land of the Ever Young should, on
conversion to Christianity, with its promise of immortality in a
state of equal blessedness, have turned back and fixed their
attention on death and the grave. This concern with mortality
and the power of the dead brings us back from the remote past
almost to the present day, for many a child remembers as an
early experience and one never to be forgotten, being taken to
a house where a relative had died 'to see the dead person'.
There was no thought of sparing a young child this harrowing
ordeal; it was accepted as a formality that must be observed.
The viewing of a corpse, not only by close relatives but by
friends and acquaintances calling to condole with the
bereaved has not long been abandoned, if indeed it has been.
'Would you like to see them?' would be asked of a visitor to a
house where some one lay dead, and the interested party
would then be conducted upstairs. Clearly the sight of the
dead and being in their presence conferred benefit on the
living, and especially on a child. The touch of the hand of a
dead man was an accepted cure for a birthmark, and there is
an account of a child having been taken to three different
houses in succession to have a birthmark touched 'by a dead
hand.' Churchyard mould, especially from a newly dug grave
was considered an effective cure in some ailments: 'A poor
woman having a child suffering from some strumous affection,
took the little one to the churchyard, and sprinkled it with
earth from a newly-made grave.' Soil taken from a grave
would also ease the passing of someone who was 'dying hard'.

The churchyard was visited on more public occasions too.
Swearing to a debt on the grave of a deceased person was once

commonly done, and until the beginning of the seventeenth
century was sanctioned by law. Where documentary evidence
was lacking, the procedure was to lie down on the grave of the
deceased with a Bible on the breast, and swear in the presence
of witnesses to the amount owed or owing. The practice was
condemned by the civil authority in 1609 as an unfair means
of settling the matter, and one whereby orphans and other
defenceless persons were liable to be deprived of their lawful
inheritance and, it was added, 'we hold it not fitting nor
Christian-like that it should hereafter be any more used.' The
church however continued to advocate its use as the most
convenient method of deciding the issue, 'being known to all'.
The church authorities must surely have looked upon the
custom as purely legal procedure, and can scarcely have
envisaged the possibility of the dead rising up from the grave
to present the true facts.

The origin of these more earthy aspects of supernatural
belief and practice can only be guessed at. Those customs
concerned with graves and corpses may represent some
remnant of a primitive people's veneration for dead ancestors
and for the places of the dead, the graves and mounds where
they were buried. It is impossible for us now to realize what
death and burial in the earth meant to the first people of the
Island, but it is fairly certain that the laying of the dead in the
ground was not merely a ceremony for the decent disposal of a
corpse, but rather a preparation for another stage in life. The
after-life was to continue in the earth itself, not in some
unknown spiritual sphere, or so it would seem, for from the
time of stone age man, and even as late as the Vikings, there
were placed with the dead in the grave, vessels, ornaments,
tools, weapons, slain animals and even human beings, all the
things they would need for a continued existence
underground. The dead did not die even in the body, but lived
on in the grave and those left behind strove to content them
with gifts and keep them from coming back to haunt them.
Though out of sight they were not forgotten, and at certain
times and seasons of the year it was believed they might
return.

The later beliefs in the power and healing virtue of corpses
and graves and the sense of a living presence in and around
the grave, is perhaps all that folk memory has retained of this
not always very peaceful after-life in, and occasionally out of,

the grave, of which full recollection has possibly been spontaneously obliterated as being too macabre to be held in mind. There is an Icelandic story of a man called Glam who even in life was not of very pleasant appearance 'his eyes were grey and gloomy and his hair was wolf-grey'. He came to work as sheep-minder at the haunted farm of Thorhallstead, undaunted by rumours of ghosts about the place. 'Such bugs will not scare me,' quoth Glam, 'life seems to me less irksome thereby.' But at Yule he disappeared and after days of searching was found dead, looking even more horrible than when he was alive, 'as blue as hell and as great as a neat'. On the ground where he lay there were signs of a great struggle, the footprints of his killer as 'big as cask-bottoms'. Even with horses to drag him he could not be brought to church for burial, so he was buried where he lay out on the hill, though he didn't rest there under his cairn. 'But ever Glam came home and rode the house-roofs'. He did more. He killed the farm-men and the livestock breaking all their bones, and murdered the farmer's daughter. He was overcome at last after a fierce fight, by Grettir the Strong who cut off his head, but not before Glam stretched out on the ground, his eyes rolling horribly upward in the moonlight, had laid a spell on him. 'This weird I lay on thee, ever to see these eyes with thine eyes, and thou wilt find it hard to be alone, and that shall drag thee to death'. After that they took no more chances with him. 'They set to work and burned Glam to cold coals and thereafter they gathered his ashes into the skin of a beast and dug it down whereas sheep-pastures were fewest, or the ways of men.'

If it was creatures such as this that haunted the old burial places, emerging out of the earth like trolls – and the Isle of Man is not without its troll place-names – animated corpses riding the roof-tops and tearing man and beast limb from limb, it is hardly any wonder that the return of the dead was deemed highly undesirable. If by any chance they were the originals of those 'fairies' for whom the door was left on the latch and who came back to the shelter of hearth and home on stormy nights, tradition has wrought a wonderful change in their appearance. Most sightings of the fairies in the Isle of Man prove them to have been of fairly presentable appearance, not as beautiful perhaps as the Irish Sidh, but without the stark horror of this Icelandic *draugr*. There was an old woman of Jurby who once had a particularly personal vision of them – 'the good people of the sunset land', she called them, claiming to have seen them playing in the rays of the setting sun, all of them with wings and one wearing a crown. These little ariels may have been on a visit here, for they were untypical of Manx fairies. However there must have been change in fairy fashion over the centuries, for tradition can select and reject, and with Glam and his like as the possible original and dreadful alternative, some transformation obviously had to take place, so that wings and crowns, those appurtenances of stage fairies, seem almost justifiable.

The attempt to trace these more sinister customs in Manx folklore back to any particular time or place or people is merely to indulge the passion of folklorists (with some almost an occupational disease) for seeking sources and derivations. Though always an interesting exercise it is seldom conclusive, and is particularly fruitless in the case of customs concerned with death and burial, which have such universal application.

This doesn't rule out all generalization and it can be justifiably assumed that some of the folk wisdom inherited from the past once belonged to a select few, whether Celtic druids or no. There is support for the assumption in the fact that certain well-known families in the Island possessed a hereditary knowledge of folk medicine which had been handed down through many generations from father to daughter and mother to son up to the end of the nineteenth century and even into this. There may be members of these families who still have this knowledge, even if they never make use of it, for it is impossible to say when such traditional matter finally dies out.

The most noted family were the Teares of Andreas, and one of them who lived and worked toward the end of the eighteenth and into the early years of the nineteenth century was highly endowed with the ancestral gift, an almost legendary figure, much venerated, and famous throughout the Island as a worker of charms and cures, both animal and human. It is just possible that several generations of the family, and even other anonymous charm-workers, may have been represented in this one man, but on *Teare Ballawhane,* undoubtedly the best remembered of them, the Druid's mantle would seem to have fallen, and to the people of the Island he was known as 'The Fairy Doctor'. He could undo the harm done by spells and the evil eye, or, if consulted in time, prevent it. His reputation as a healer of sickness in farm animals was quite consonant with this, as the affliction was rarely believed to be from natural causes, but was almost invariably attributed to the evil eye, the fairy stroke or witchcraft. Teare was in great demand in spring when farmers were preparing to sow their corn, to come and put his own kind of benediction on the fields as sowing could not be safely undertaken until he had done so. The historian Joseph Train gives a picture of 'the seer Teare', as he calls him: 'a little man far advanced into the vale of life, in appearance healthy and active, wearing a low-crowned slouch hat evidently too large for his head, with a broad brim ... and breeches and stockings of undyed Manx wool.' Train states that in his hearing the charmer swore an oath at the request of a magistrate, that he 'never called evil spirits to his assistance', and gives also an instance of his control over the depredations of birds, which was one of his special gifts. Teare had been sent for by Mr Faragher an innkeeper of Laxey to put a charm on his cornfield where sparrows were eating the ripening grain. There were some sceptics in the village at this time among the paper-makers and miners who had doubts about the fairy doctor's powers, so they carefully observed the behaviour of the sparrows after he had worked on the field and saw 'to their great surprise, though they flocked round Mr Faragher's park in greater numbers than before ... yet not one of them dared to enter the charmed precincts.'

The way in which the sage of Andreas set about curing illness in a human being shows that he not only had knowledge of the herbs themselves, but also understood the significance of numbers in the quantities used in preparation and dosage. He prescribed as follows:

he said the words over the cut herbs and then divided them into three parts, about a small handful in each part. Each of these was divided into three and to each one a cup of boiling water was put, and then left to draw for nine minutes. The sick man was to take nine teaspoonfuls of the stuff or put the teaspoon nine times to his lips. This small part was to be put into use every third night until the whole of the parts were used. The length of time gave him time to get better. Then his face and every part of his body was to be washed with the leavings, and if there was any over it was to be cast into the fire.

At the time when Train was writing in 1843, he notes that, though 'the fairies had left the Island in rum-puncheons ... in the direction of Jamaica, Fairy Doctors continue to be employed in the Island' and mentions one at Ballasalla, and Teare, as the most famous, the latter 'a very extensive dealer in propitiatory charms and in antidotes to occult infection ... the messenger that is despatched to him on such occasions is neither to eat nor to drink by the way, nor even to tell any person his mission. The recovery is said to be peceptible from the time the case is stated to him.'

Among women practitioners, who incidentally do not seem to have been known as fairy doctors but as herb women or simply by name (though occasionally it has to be admitted as witches), the most noted was Nan Wade, whose name like Teare's was a charm in itself. A course of treatment by her was a rather uncanny experience, especially to a child:

> I remember being brought to Nan's once when I was very young. I was what they called donsay – delicate. I was very much frightened. I had heard that Nan was a witch and could do what she liked with people. Silver was given by the woman who took me to her and Nan covered it with salt and threw the salt into a saucer containing something like pinjean [junket]. She then rubbed her fore-finger in the earthen floor just under where I stood and dipping it into the saucer crossed my forehead, chin, palms of the hands and tip of the tongue with her wet forefinger, muttering low in Manx to herself all the time. I think this crossing was repeated three times, more than once anyhow. Before she began the charm, everybody in the room was turned out, just leaving myself, a trembling mite and her together, and I was strictly enjoined not to utter a word during its performance. When she had finished she threw the contents of the saucer on the turf burning in the chiollagh.

The person who recalled this childhood visit to Nan Wade gave also a word of advice about the use of herbs. 'Herb-charmers never spoke of picking herbs but always of lifting them, and the herb had to be lifted with a charm. The sick person had to have the herbs lifted especially for them, the same lifting would not do in more than one case. The use of nine different pieces of the herb was most potent, then seven, six was good and three would serve if the plant was scarce.'

Men and woman like these have been spoken of as 'the last of the druids' and whether they deserved the title or no, they were certainly regarded with respect, and their help was sought in all cases of illness, and often in misfortune. The charmers and folk doctors were called in when cholera broke out in the 1830s, and the qualified medical men found themselves unwanted. There was even a rumour in circulation at the time that they were responsible for the fever as they had 'poisoned the springs', the public water supply, and the people became very hostile towards them. Lack of faith in orthodox medical science and an age-old reliance on the fairy doctors and herb-women were probably accountable for people's reluctance to undergo vaccination for smallpox which also occurred in epidemic form later in the nineteenth century.

This clash of opinion between ancient and modern in medicine, the 'druids versus the doctors' perhaps, though not the 'qualified versus the quacks' the folk doctors were never thought of in those terms, came to a head towards the middle of last century, when in 1844 local medical men proposed that a medical Bill be introduced into the Manx Legislature to regulate the practice of medicine in the Island, requiring all druggists and apothecaries to be licensed, thus eliminating the unqualified. It was a proposal aimed of course at the 'country doctors' and at the whole practice of folk medicine.

The people were very indignant at the prospect of the medical monopoly the Bill envisaged and at the likelihood of being deprived of the cheap, usually free, medical advice they had always had recourse to. So strong was their resentment that they rose in protest, parish by parish. Public meetings were called, whose spokesmen declared the new Bill to be 'altogether uncalled for and unnecessary, and if passed into law', likely to be 'highly prejudicial to the interests of the inhabitants of the Isle in general'. There were vehement expressions of faith in the country doctors, whom the Medical profession, by the introduction of the Bill hoped to put out of practice. The people asserted that 'many of the inhabitants of this Isle have had their health restored and their limbs preserved unto them by the agency of 'country doctors'.

The Bill took no effect at this time, the time was not ripe, for the day of the country doctors was not yet done. They continued to be in demand for many years to come, and were not deprived of status until 1899 when a long-deferred medical Bill was introduced and became law.

4 Witchcraft – The Black Art

IT IS NO USE attempting to claim that witchcraft in the Isle of Man was nothing more than an inherited folk wisdom concerning itself mostly with the art of healing, or that its dealings in the occult were quite innocuous. It had its darker side.

The true and comparatively recent practitioner of the black art was called a *buitch,* probably the English word witch Gaelicised: their craft and its harmful result were known as *buitcheragh,* a word similarly derived, and both conveying in their very sound the sly malice and evil designing mind with which a witch was credited. Before and during the seventeenth and eighteenth centuries, though witches may have been just as evil and black-hearted, the words buitch and buitcheragh were not in such common use. Their calling was ennobled by a far finer-sounding name. When Jony a witch of Kirk Braddan, notorious in her day met a woman coming along the road one dark night, her reply to the startled inquiry 'Who's there?' was haughty and far from reassuring: *She mish y ven-obbee vooar ta ayn'* ('It is I, the great enchantress that's in'). There seem to have been recognised grades in wizardry and magic, and the Manx language makes distinction between *Fir as Mraane Obbee,* men and women of Enchantment, and *Fyssereee* of Knowledge, wise men and women. The stock in trade of the witch, the worker of evil and of the fairy doctor who was able to dispel it seem in the course of time to have become inextricably mixed. Both kinds of practitioner made use of many objects, amulets and talismans for protection and cure; coins, rings and pins and bits of thread, bones, twigs and stones to be carried about or worn, and they had written charms and murmured incantations to be read or said over a patient while a cure was being performed, and though many of them were used for healing purposes, they could be used in a quite opposite way to bring affliction.

The ambiguous nature of the charm itself is shown in the simple and fairly common cure prescribed for warts, which was to rub them with a piece of stolen meat (secrecy was essential in all charms, so it must be stolen) then bury the meat in the ground, and as it decayed the warts would disappear. This process could be put to a sinister purpose, though the details of the performance were almost identical. 'A piece of flesh would be buried in the ground in order to go rotten in order to do harm to a man or beast.' As the meat decomposed the person or animal the charm was designed to injure would slowly waste away. In one account of the performance of this charm, there was an actual interment in the cemetery, the meat that was intended to cause physical wasting in the victim was placed in a box as in a coffin, and a burial service was read over the 'grave'.

Of less tangible ways used by the buitch to inflict harm on their victims little is known as most of their work was done in secret. They had the power to afflict as the charmer could cure, from a distance. This special ability of witches 'to strike unknown' or 'unawares' was one of their most dreaded characteristics: it was an indictable offence in the ecclesiastical courts to which there was no lack of witnesses to testify. 'Ann Cowle, sworn examined, saith that John Steon said unto her he would deceive her and blind her and strike her unknown. Adam Callister ... said that the said Steon told him he would strike him unawares and John Corlett said that that was the common report he had heard of John Steon, that he would strike people unknown.'

The fear of witchcraft, of an unseen power working in secret yet known to be of human agency, made people distrust and suspect each other. The innocent were as open to suspicion as the guilty and any old woman living alone was liable to be considered a witch. If a child or an animal fell sick, the illness was scarcely ever thought to be from purely physical causes, but was assumed to be the result of *buitcheragh,* the evil eye cast on a child by someone who had been in the house, or an ill-wish on the cattle by a passer-by, and there had to be immediate recourse to the appropriate counteracting ritual. Sweeping the road and shovelling up the dust from under the evil-doer's footsteps was the remedy oftenest resorted to, and throwing the dust over the afflicted creature. This cure continued to be put into practice within comparatively recent years, as a last resource when all else had failed, by people who normally would never have used it.

My father told me once that he had a cow that took sick. She just lay down in the stall and wouldn't get up and was eatin' hardly at all. He was a middlin' religious man and takin' no notice of what some ones were sayin' about beasts bein' grudged (bewitched), but for all that he went out with the shovel to the end of the road and brushed up the dust where the people was passin' and threw it over the cow, for there was no sign of her gettin' better with the drench he was givin' her. As he said himself, 'Even if it'll do her no good, it's like it'll do her no harm neither'. An' whether it was the dust or not she took a turn soon after, and wasn' long till she was on her feet.

'Dus' from the footsteps' was the most widely accepted panacea and after that, fire. Fire was a most potent antidote against witchcraft and would purify a place from its influences and nullify the effects of a witch's spells, and in certain special circumstances make the witch reveal herself, or as was quite often the case, himself. Both these motives lay behind the many instances that occurred of lighting bonfires to burn the carcases of farm livestock that died. Outbreaks of cattle disease were by no means uncommon, and many animals died. Some farmers whose cattle were struck down by some mysterious 'murrain' believed that, if they burned the carcase of a beast that died, this would check the spread of the disease in the remainder of the herd. Whether there was any element of sacrifice in this performance is a point on which folklorists disagree. The more conscientious point out that as the animal was already dead, burning its body hardly constituted a 'sacrifice', but others were greatly taken with the idea of a burnt offering to some god.

When the carcase was burning in the bonfire, it was believed that the witch or suspected person would appear in the smoke, and some held that this was the chief purpose of the burning, to bring the buitch to the spot; the fire drew him irresistibly and 'he had to come'. A story is told of some men who were fishing off the Kirk Michael coast, when one of them suddenly announced that he couldn't stay out any longer but must go ashore. The other men were very reluctant to leave off to take him in as they were doing well and fish were plentiful and they refused to go. He became more and more agitated and threatened at last to jump overboard if they wouldn't do as he wished, so they gave in and made for the shore. After they had landed him they watched for a while and saw him start to run in the direction of a field where a bonfire was blazing fiercely in a corner of it down near the sea. It was a farmer burning an animal that had died. Whether he had anyone in mind when he chose the site for his bonfire no-one knew, but it drew the fisherman like a magnet. He was the buitch and 'he had to go'.

It was commonly believed here as in many other places that a witch could take the form of a hare, and stories of hares turning into old women and vice versa could once be heard in every parish. Sabine Baring-Gould mentions a folk belief that witches are transformed after death into hares and adds 'a lady wrote to me from the Isle of Man that she could not get her servants to eat hare because it might be the body of some old woman transformed'. This evidently was the form in which Baring-Gould found the belief, but in the many Manx stories based on it, both witch and hare are very much alive, and no matter where the story is told the details vary little. Someone seeing a hare disappear over a hedge would later find an old woman walking about on the other side of it, or the hare might be shot and wounded in the leg – but never fatally unless with a silver bullet as ammunition – and then sometime later a woman suspected of being a witch would be seen walking with a limp.

An unusual slant is given to the belief in a story from Ballafesson in the south of the Island, the witch in this case being a man. This 'witchman' came into a house one day where a man was mending nets, and as he watched he started talking in a curious way about the fields at Cregneash: he spoke of certain fields where the grass was very sweet, and of others where it had a bitter taste. The man who was listening to him supposed that he was remembering how the grass tasted when he had been eating it in all the different fields at Cregneash in the form of a hare.

This particular witch propensity attributed to some people was known in the Isle of Man as being 'rough under the foot'. The man who supplied this invaluable piece of information said that up to a few years ago the use of the expression in company was a guaranteed conversation stopper: not as might be the case today that it was not understood, but because it was understood only too well. He recalls hearing it used once quite openly when he was having dinner in a farmhouse. Some neighbours who had come to help in the hay were sitting round the table with the family, and conversation was brisk. Then suddenly someone remarked of a man whose name had been mentioned 'they used to say he was a bit rough under the foot', and at once there was dead silence and everyone looked embarassed. It was not the kind of thing to say out loud and in company; only when two or three were gathered together could it be spoken of with any propriety, and better then in a whisper.

Charles Roeder, possibly with the idea of clearing the matter up in his own mind, once drew up a very comprehensive list of Gaelic witchcraft terms in current use at the end of last century in the Isle of Man, expressions designating the various practices and practitioners of the art in all their shades and grades of meaning, differentiating the *pishag*, or spell, from the *rhusag*, the amulet, and distinguishing between the *Fer Druiaght*, the wizard, and the *Caillagh ny Gueshag*, the witch of the spells. For the most part his terms of enchantment are credible enough, but one or two like the *cowrey druiaght,* the sign or symbol of wizardry, and the *cloagey druiaght,* the cloak of invisibility, read more like the language of fairy tale, and an Irish fairy tale rather than a Manx one, which is possibly where Roeder found them: expressions that may once have been used here, but of which the language preserves no record. The dictionaries of Manx Gaelic, rich in obscure technical and idiomatic words and phrases, fall rather short on the romantic and poetic, so that at first one is inclined regretfully to reject Roeder's terms for the more esoteric aspects of sorcery as expressions we should like to have and possibly ought to have since they were part of the art-magic of the past and of Manannan, but to which we can no longer lay claim. However going back two or three hundred years in the records, there is a case of a woman who was accused of concocting a brew from certain plants which, if drunk, 'would make a man forget himself and if he drank of it twice he would forget himself for ever'. If this was the way people talked before the ecclesiastical court when they were being arraigned for their so-called sins, and though in danger of imprisonment and excommunication were yet capable of such turns of phrase, Roeder's cloak of invisibility seems a slightly less improbable garment.

When occasion called for it, witches made use of a kind of utterance that must once have been as powerful as any weapon in their armoury, the curse. Manx people generally, speaking in their native Gaelic had a fervour and eloquence that deserted them to a large extent when they adopted English. In the Gaelic they spoke with dignity, using an idiom of which they had a natural mastery. The Anglo-Manx dialect, a hybrid tongue made up of expressions and idioms translated straight out of the Gaelic mixed up with imported elements, is an entirely different kind of speech, and though by now characteristic of the people and entirely Manx in feeling it is still something that has been grafted on, not the original growth. The Gaelic language persisted through every phase of the Island's changing history; even the Norsemen couldn't change the way the people spoke. To lose a language as the Manx people have done, and adopt an entirely new form of expression must have caused a radical change in the people themselves, in their manner of thought and their attitudes. It marked a complete break with the past and created a gap, especially in the transmission of oral tradition, which has never been bridged. Across it our ancestors are like a foreign people whom we can never really know, nor how they sounded as they talked together in the language that had evolved from ancient Gaelic speech.

This was the language of the witch's curse, and in pronouncing it she exercised that gift for rhetoric which Celtic peoples are said to possess. The old Methodist preachers did likewise, and earned themselves a reputation for eloquence, in English eventually as well as in their native Manx. Their preaching was influenced by the language of the Bible, and they cultivated particularly the art of prayer, of which the technique seems to have been well understood. It was something in the manner of the Welsh *hwyl,* a gradual build-up in tone and intensity, the rule being

> Begin slow, keep low.
> Rise higher and take fire.

Though it seems almost blasphemous to suggest it, it is possible that both types of eloquence were rooted in a common origin. The preachers, who were spoken of as 'powerful in prayer', inherited their gift of utterance from predecessors who had an equivalent power in cursing, of whom the witches were direct descendants.

It is significant that the word *guee* in Manx means both to pray and to curse, and both forms of imprecation were performed in the same attitude, on the knees. In 1722 a woman was presented in the court for wishing that the curse of God would fall upon her neighbour's colt, and for 'wishing upon her knees' that his goods would never thrive. Women were always wishing on their knees, and expressions like 'thou leprous perjur'd thief', 'ye offspring of witches', or 'an ill hour to thine eyes' sprang to their lips without any prompting. A woman driving an obstinate sheep wished the devil to take it off the face of the earth, and another prayed that as many devils would tear the soul of Captain C—— of Ramsey, as he had sent beasts of theirs to the pinfold, and a third that a man might burn in his own corn-kiln. The Church Court records are full of the language of cursing: the curse of God, of the devil, of the King of Easter, called down indiscriminately on neighbours, enemies, parsons, husbands, servants and animals, even butchers 'may the devil take the half of them'.

The church wardens who took exception to it and made the presentments of offenders called it 'most scandalous and bitter cursing'. Sheer bad temper and irritability could hardly account for such poisonous utterance, no matter how exasperating the circumstances that provoked it. The more one reads of it, the more there is heard the echo of a professional voice, a ritual performance: 'may the curse of God go along with his bones into the grave, that keeps us together. *Skeab lome* to his door, and where he lies'. The Manx language has preserved certain dire forms of malediction whose original intent to blast and destroy can now only be surmised, though the words themselves still hold a powerful ring of menace. Of these, the superlative curse, the fine flower of cursing so to speak in the Manx Gaelic were the *shiaght mynney mollaght,* the seven bitter curses, and the ritual curse of the *skeab lome,* the naked broom. The sevenfold curse eventually lost its venom, and came to be used in a general exclamatory fashion, as when a certain John Cowle sent a wish after a departing curate that 'his seven curses might go along with him and follow him', but the original ritual was performed with great deliberation, accompanied by the turning of a swearing stone, and said to have taken place secretly at night on Tynwald hill. It was the 'Loo Mynney Mollaght,' the bitter curse, that leaves neither root nor branch that Young Orree not surprisingly was moved to utter when he found himself tied to the harrows by the jealous daughters of Fin and Oshin, who had also set a train of fire to his feet: his reaction according to the ancient fragment of Manx verse that recounts it was to swear another oath, by the sun and the moon, to burn them and their houses to the ground. In the Mylecharane ballad, the old miser had the curse put on him for providing his daughter with a marriage dowry:

> *My hiaght mynney mollaght ort, Vylecharane*
> *Son uss va'n chied ghooiney hug toghyr da mraane.*
> My seven bitter curses on thee Mylecharane
> For thou wast the first to give dowry to women.

Sentiments that were justifiable at the time, since this innovation meant a complete reversal of fortune for a prospective bride's father, as it had previously been the custom for the bridegroom to bring the marriage portion.

To wish *skeab lome* to a person even in the short form in which the curse was sometimes found was to desire total annihilation to fall on them, the naked broom standing as a symbol of the power that was to sweep them out of existence. The scope and range of a witch's curse is given at some length in a dialect poem of T. E. Brown, The Manx Witch, of which the following extract is only part

Cussin' your fingers and cussin' your toes
Cussin' your mouth and cussin' your nose,
Every odd joint an' every limb
And all your inside – that's the trim,
Cussin' your horse an cussin' your cow,
Cussin' your boar an cussin' your sow,
Everything that's got a tail,
Aye, and your spade and your cart and your flail,
Plough and harra's, stock and crop,
Nets and lines – they'll never stop ...

The curse of the *skeab lome* pronounced in its entirety covers as much ground, and far more succinctly and in fact going further: *'Skeab lome ort hene, er dty hollagh, er dty hlaynt, er dty chooid as er dty Chloan ... follym faase, gyn cass, gyn rass'* ('... on thyself, on thy hearth, thy health, on thy goods and children ... an empty desolation, without root or seed').

The malevolence of the witch in Brown's lines was plain for all to see; he painted her as black as she was, but there was another and equally characteristic kind of witch personality with an apparent smoothness of speech and manner that never quite managed to hide the inner blackness. W. W. Gill seems to have been well acquainted with this subtler aspect of witch psychology and dwells on his recollection of it in a voice he remembered: ' "Deed she has and deed she was", it comes back to me, that caressing suavity as a characteristic of the sisterhood. It is superficial, and never lulls one's uneasy sense of a deadly undercurrent belying the smooth surface.'

The only Manx witch celebrated by name in Manx literary tradition is *Berrey Dhone,* Brown Berrey, who belonged to Kirk Maughold, a parish with more surviving witch lore than any other, and there is a ballad about her in the Manx language. The anonymous writer of it possibly for reasons of discretion understandable in matters of this kind, fails to be at all explicit, merely hinting at her activities and giving no clue to her identity. Perhaps because of his reticence in providing biographical and scandalous detail there is little of the malicious evil-hearted witch about the figure he describes, and she remains enshrined in it, a rather splendid though enigmatic Amazon of a woman striding over the mountains of three parishes and likely to be met with by late-returning turf-cutters. There was some blot on her character but whatever she was guilty of, and whatever her deserts, she escaped hanging.

> She went to the gallows,
> But she found favour there,
> And came back by Mullagh Ouyr
> Leading home a goat.

If she came as near to hanging as the ballad suggests, there should be some recognisable mention of her in the records, but her existence outside Manx ballad literature seems unproven. It is even more remarkable that a mid-nineteenth-century writer of verse, William Kennish, who belonged to Kirk Maughold and wrote mainly about the traditions of his own parish, should have nothing to say about her, although one of his longer poems, *Old May Eve,* could almost be called a treatise on witchcraft practice in his part of the Island, the Cornaa valley which lies under the shadow of North Barrule, the mountain around which the traditions of this the most famous of all Kirk Maughold witches seem to centre. When Kennish was writing, the belief in withcraft was still very much alive, so unless he was exercising his talents in re-creating what he had heard at second-hand, he was probably writing from his own knowledge and experience. He described a witch cult that seemed to have had no parallel anywhere else in the island, so that apart from one or two inconclusive scraps of information gleaned here and there, his poems, especially *May Eve,* constitute the only strong evidence that witch assemblies were ever held in the Isle of Man. Without these verses, there would be little to support the notion fostered by one folklorist in particular and based chiefly on Berrey Dhone tradition, that there was 'a graded corpus of witches' of which Berrey was the head, whose seat of learning was on the sunnier side of North Barrule, even inside it. It is typical of Walter Gill, whose theory this is, to suggest that Berrey was not a human witch at all, but similar to the Irish and Scottish mountain hag, the Scots Gaelic *Cailleach Bheur,* and not living on the mountain, but buried under the cairn there, and haunting the surrounding hills; like her Celtic counterparts associated with animals, and with a witch's ability to influence the weather. Comparisons like this are admissible enough though Berrey had not many of the Cailleach's qualities, but she had a double or a familiar in the form of an ox, so there may be something in Gill's suggestion, and as he says, her rather unusual taste in headgear, *lhiack er e kione,* a stone on her head (mentioned in one verse of her ballad), might be the stone of the cairn she lies under. However Berrey Dhone emerges from Gill's speculations about her a more baffling figure than before. He begins with a live witch being admitted into the mountain by her subordinates, and ends with her lying dead under it, with myths and legends flocking round her like carrion crows.

Not so William Kennish: he was nothing if not factual and circumstantial, yet in spite of the convincing impression he gives of having been an eye witness of the proceedings he describes, they are so totally different from witch rites observed anywhere else in the Isle of Man, that it might almost be supposed that he invented the scenes he ascribed to the southern end of his native parish; if it were not that is for his footnotes. Surely footnotes are an indication of authenticity, and imagined scenes would hardly require them. Of the place-name Creg-ny-Mhuilt he says that it was 'an eminence ... famed of old for being the haunt of the higher grade of witches'. Of the different witch grades he appears to have a special knowledge, and speaks of others 'on probation ere they were allowed to take high degrees in witchcraft'. His witches are real enough: one of them, old Kate, seems to embody the whole range of witch characteristics in her own person. She is the convener of the Maughold coven and organiser of their tactics and forays (it reads like the report of a military operation). But apart from her corporate responsibilities Old Kate did a fair amount of *jeel* on her own initiative, especially to fishermen:

At her command the gobogs dole [the blind dog-fish]
would rend the nets in many a hole,

And liberate the herring shoal.
She'd raise the wind with sudden blast
And leave the boat without a mast;
And drive her on the leeward shore
To perish mid the breakers' roar.
Indeed 'twas said she could outdo
Old Nick himself, and all his crew.

If Kennish's account can be relied on and has an actual basis in tradition, it is of particular interest since it contains the only really circumstantial evidence of what the witches did on May Eve, the great early summer Festival of Beltain, when they were known to be at the height of their power, and the time when the strongest measures were taken against them. The customs of May Eve intended to protect flocks and herds and crops and the whole house and farmstead from witchcraft on this night were well remembered, and even yet people can recall the lighting of bonfires and the strewing around of flowers, but it seems as if he somehow got behind the veil of secrecy that shrouded the witches' working methods, and observed them preparing themselves for the occasion

Ere chanticleer, with clarion shrill
Would break the enchantment of the gill,
Where sat old Nick in state that night,
He and his suite took to their flight.
And left old Kate in full possession
Of his black art, and at discretion
To initiate those upon probation
And give each hag her proper station.
Tho' first she'd Hornie to consult
Who best t'appoint to Crag na Mult,
Being the most important post
On all Kirk Maughold's warlock coast.
Now Kate to each her post decreed,
And all assembled had agreed
To put their witchcraft to the test,
And for their master do their best.

There is further slight evidence for this habit of witches taking counsel together on May Eve to work out a plan of campaign. In Ballaugh, men from other parishes used to meet on the bridge 'to devise witchcraft for their parishes for the rest of the year'. As for allegiance to Old Nick though it's not a thing that would be readily confessed to perhaps, for one woman in old age it was a rather dimmed memory. Her own mother was a witch and when she felt her powers failing she initiated her daughter with her personal gifts in the art by a kind of unholy baptism. The daughter, recalling the ceremony she underwent as a girl, appearing to have forgotten most of it but she remembered swearing an oath 'to give up all belief in the Almighty's power, and trust in that of the evil one instead'. Kennish has his higher-grade witches doing this, and as they became more experienced, achieving a nice balance between their commitment to the devil and their duty to their neighbours, each of them resolved to end the strife

> Existing twixt her and mankind,
> And set to work her crafty mind
> How best both parties she could please.

To save their own skins from silver bullets and other inconveniences these Manx witches allied themselves with the fairies, who were apparently of a very small variety and could execute the witches designs without hazard to themselves.

In only three cases is it on record that Manx witches were condemned to death, and of these one was reprieved: but in 1617 Margaret Ine Quane and her son who was implicated with her in a conviction for witchcraft of which no details remain were burned in the market place at Castletown.

Slieau Whallian, whose sharp slope rises up almost from the foot of Tynwald hill in the centre of the Island, is always pointed out as the mountain where witches were punished by being rolled down its side in spiked barrels. Of this tradition dating from remote, possibly from Viking times there is happily no instance that can be cited, though a local story that on stormy nights a human voice can be heard howling in the wind along the mountainside believed to be that of a murdered witch, proves that there is a surviving memory in the neighbourhood of Slieau Whallian of the agonies suffered there by poor wretches in the distant past. The punishment meted out was according to tradition even more diabolical, the barrel ride being only its final stage. A witch, once she was convicted, had no hope: she was thrown into the Curragh

Glass, the swamp at the foot of the mountain, and if she managed to float and emerge alive, she proved herself a witch and was given the ultimate punishment, death by burning or in the spiked barrel. If she drowned, she was shown to be innocent of the charge of witchcraft, but had no profit of her innocence in this world, even though she 'was taken home and waked and given a Christian burial'.

Apart from such traditionally based stories of punishment and the two known cases of execution, the worst penalties suffered by women convicted of witchcraft were a fine as in the case of Elizabeth Black, or imprisonment, or a sentence of penance, which required them to stand at the church door or at the market cross of the Island's towns draped in a white sheet, holding a white wand in the right hand, and the words 'For Witchcraft and Sorcery' in capital letters on their breast. To this latter punishment Alice Knakill was condemned when in 1712 she was found guilty of taking earth from under her neighbour's door, burning it, then giving the ash to her own cattle to make them give more milk. She also prescribed a love potion for a young man in the form of a powder 'of some of the bright stones that are at Foxdale'.

In some instances the judge of the court exercised his discretion and appeared not to take the charge too seriously, which though it showed good sense was a highly individual approach to a charge of witchcraft in those days, when the prevailing attitude was rather more that of the scriptural injunction 'Thou shalt not suffer a witch to live'. In the early years of the seventeenth century the Vicar of Braddan who as Vicar-General presided over the Ecclesiastical Court, had brought before him an old woman with a previous reputation as a witch, who was alleged to have said, 'Give me a pair of new pewter dishes which have never been used and I will convert them into wings and fly across the channel from the Isle of Man to Scotland.' The Vicar-General chose to disregard the rumours about her, and dismissed the case saying that in his view there was 'no law against a woman flying from the Isle of Man to Scotland'. This mode of travel, unlikely as it may seem, was not unknown in the Island; Manx witches on the whole from the rather scanty available evidence were more given to propulsion through the air by means of a *saagh,* a vessel, than on the more conventional (if that is the word) broomstick.

5 Life and Death

HOWEVER MUCH PEOPLE CONCERNED themselves with the fairy world, and it was a subject that was never far from their minds, as long as they confined themselves to talking about fairies and passed their time telling the old stories about them, there was little that could be done to draw them away from their age-old beliefs, and it is doubtful if this was a matter of much concern to those responsible for their moral welfare. The church seems to have been much more preoccupied with witchcraft and to have considered it a far greater evil, compared to which it has been said the fairies might well have been regarded as 'a harmless dream'. This apparent lack of opposition to fairy belief is surprising as there were certain occasions when the dream was translated into overt action to which the church might have been expected to object, and one of these was the birth of a child.

The conduct of everyday life was strictly supervised by the church, the self-appointed arbiter in matters of public and especially of private morality, and at its special occasions – birth, marriage and death – opportunities arose and were frequently seized upon to exercise its authority and counteract and control the tendency to stray into forbidden paths, and to punish those who offended. From the day of birth right through life until they died people were under the watchful eye of the church and its officials, and answerable to them for the conduct of their most personal and intimate affairs.

As early as the thirteenth century church law had stressed the necessity for baptism: 'Let Chaplains beware lest through neglect any infant die without baptism (which God forbid)'. The rite was one that with the visiting of the sick and the burial of the dead was to be administered freely without 'fee or reward'. Not that parents showed any reluctance to having their children baptised; on the contrary, to be deprived of it for any reason was a source of grief and anxiety to them, as they believed that if a child died without baptism it would not go to heaven. When in the seventeenth century the Clergy had become lax in the performance of their duties, the people complained: 'the sick are not visited; parties dying without prayers, exhortations and the Holy Communion, though much desired by the sick. Children weak and strong have to be taken to other parishes for their christendom and to pay for it'.

The church authorities must have been well aware that at the time of a child's birth, and before its baptism, certain other measures were taken to promote its safety. The new-born child was never taken out of the house nor left alone in it, or if the woman left in charge of it had to go out of the room, fire-irons, often the tongs, or tongs and poker of smithy forged iron, were placed cross-wise over the child's cradle. Salt was put in the child's mouth to give it protection, or a spot of soot was daubed on its arm. An offering of food was made to ward off evil, as it was believed that if food was given to someone who intended to harm the new-born infant, their intention was averted: it was customary therefore in a house where a baby was expected to have plenty of bread and cheese ready to offer to all comers. The food was called by the very un-Manx sounding name of 'blithe meat', though Hall Caine in one of his novels introduces the custom and uses this expression as if it were current speech. In *The Deemster* Thorkill Mylrea at the birth of his son rouses his servant and sets him to break the oatcake and cheese into small pieces in the 'peck' and when this was done, to scatter it broadcast on the stairs and landing, and on the garden path in front of the house, while he himself carried a similar peck, piled up like a pyramid with pieces of oatcake and cheese, to the room whence there issued at intervals a thin, small voice, which was the sweetest music that had even yet fallen on Thorkill's ear ... Then throughout three long jovial weeks the visitors came and went, and every day the 'blithe bread' was piled in the peck for the poor of the earth, and scattered on the paths for the good spirits of the air.

It seems unlikely that the Gaelic-speaking people of the Island would have spoken of 'blithe meat', though the inmates of the Deemster's house might have done so. It is more convincing to find it called simply *arran as caashey*, bread and cheese; people used to say *'Bee arran as caashey ec Balla – dy-gherrid'* ('There'll be bread and cheese at Balla – soon'). The mention of the scattering of the food for 'the good spirits of the air' possibly places the custom in the right context, as some kind of placatory offering.

As it was necessary for the child's well-being to take this defensive action on its behalf until it was safely baptised, *arran as caashey* were also taken along by a woman taking a child to church for baptism, and offered to those she met on the way. There was a man in Kirk Maughold who from his habit of making himself comfortable in haystacks was known as *Ned Lag y Thurran,* Ned of the Hollow of the Stack, and he used to lie in wait by the side of the church road on the chance of meeting a woman bringing a child to be baptised, as he knew that she would be sure to give him some of the bread and cheese she had in her pocket.

At the beginning of life and at its end people were very much aware of the lurking presence of supernatural powers, and the new-born and the dying were believed to be particularly vulnerable to their influence. They were on the threshold between the worlds, and their coming into it and going out presented opportunities to those who were so to speak waiting in the wings. For it is some such lying in wait that seems to have characterised the behaviour of the fairies when a child was to be born. They appeared as if from nowhere, with every intention of stealing the new-born infant, though why they were so anxious to get it and what they intended to do with it is a debatable point.

There is a story told of a woman lying in bed with her new-born baby beside her, resting but quite wide awake, when suddenly the door of the bedroom opened and two tiny very old women came into the room and right up to the bedside. Before the mother could do anything to protect her baby they grabbed hold of it and tried to take it away from her, one little old woman urging *'Gow ee, gow ee!'* ('take her, take her!') and the other answering as she tugged the baby by the heel, *'Cha jargym, cha jargym!'* ('I can't, I can't!'). In the struggle they upset a jug of water that was standing on a table by the bedside and the woman cried out *'Jee jean myghin orrym!'* ('God have mercy on me!'), and immediately the old women ran out through the door. The person who told this story said that the child in it lived to be quite old herself, and all her life had finger-marks on her heel where the fairy woman had gripped her.

The concern of the clergy with baptism was on purely Christian grounds; it was a child's only hope of salvation in the next world. To the people it was also a means of protecting it from the thieving designs of the fairies. In the belief in Manx tradition that a child dying without baptism was an outcast, unable to enter heaven, but doomed to wander in limbo, carrying in its hand 'a perpetual light resembling a candle', the emphasis is as much on the naming of the child as on its baptism into the Christian faith. The story of the Child of Eary Cushlin tells of an illegitimate child born to the heiress of the farm, that died or was done away with and buried in or near the old churchyard of Lag ny Keeilley. Fishermen out fishing in the bay at night used to hear the sound of a child crying, and see a light moving about on the cliff. Many of them were afraid, but one man thought it would be better to try 'to put rest on the child', so one night when he was out alone in his boat and heard the child wailing on the shore, he called to it and asked it 'what for it was crying' and the answer came back *'She lhiannoo beg dyn ennym mee'* ('I am a little child without a name'). The fisherman stood up in his boat and said, 'If thou are a girl I name thee Joney, and if thou are a boy I name thee Juan', and after that the child seemed to be at peace, and the fishermen never heard it crying again nor saw its light on Eary Cushlin shore.

It seems as if names were of as much importance in the human as in the fairy world: there it will be recalled, knowledge of a person's name gave power over its owner, and to answer when summoned by name was to be lost to this world. In Icelandic saga the personal name held great power and virtue. The name of a recently dead relative given to a child conferred on it something of the personality of its former owner, and the bestowal of it on a child arose out of a belief in 'the connection between name-giving and the rebirth of the dead into the family'. It would scarcely be surprising to find some vestige of this Norse-derived name-lore persisting in the Isle of Man. This is not to suggest that the idea of a rebirth of the dead through the continued use of a personal name is or ever was known to have been accepted by Manx people, but the Church's insistence on baptism and the preoccupation with it in popular tradition suggests that it was regarded as a counter-measure to a non-Christian claim that might be made on the child. Whoever the church may have regarded as the rival claimants, the people had no doubt of their identity; it was the fairies who were always trying to steal away human children and substitute some of their own kind instead. The changeling left in place of a human child had no appearance of childhood but looked 'ugly and wizened', 'rough like an old man', 'all skin and bone'. It is sometimes suggested that the fairies who crowded round the threshold of a house where a child was to be born were the spirits of the dead seeking re-entry into the human world. Fairy stories can be given many meanings, but it needs no great effort of imagination to suppose that the fairies, so avidly interested in the birth of a child and so persistent in their attempts to steal it, had once been human themselves.

It was believed in the Isle of Man as in many seafaring communities that a child born with a caul would never drown, and it was considered very lucky to have one when at sea or at the fishing. A man who as a baby was born with one took it with him when he went fishing, and kept it hidden away in his boat. Another fisherman who once happened to see it said it was full of dead bees. This was an instance of a very potent combination of two customs and two lucky objects, for Manx fishermen were in the habit of trying to catch the first bee they saw in April before the herring fishing, as they believed it would bring them good luck and good catches. This man had been doing this for many years and storing the bees he caught in the caul to ensure his luck at the fishing and his safety when at sea.

The state of the tide influenced both birth and death. In the natural course of things a child would tend to be born when the tide was flowing and the aged be likely to die at the ebb, but if by an unlucky chance a child was born at low water in the time of *roayrt*, spring tide, it was considered to have an unfavourable start in life, and would never prosper.

If an infant was sick and likely to die people used to visit a cave on the coast between Fleshwick Bay and Bradda Head. It was called Ghaw Ving because it had an echo – *bing* in Manx is used of a sweet, high, even shrill note of music. For the benefit of the sick child it was necessary to go inside and call out to some invisible presence:

> *Ghaw Ving, Ghaw Ving,*
> *Cur jeed yn troo;*
> *Va'n lhiannoo ching jea,*
>   *As bee eh ny share jiu.*
> Ghaw Ving, Ghaw Ving,
>   Put off the envy,
> The child was sick yesterday
> And he'll be better today.

Some think that this invocation made on behalf of a sick child was addressed to the Cughtagh, the spirit that inhabited sea-caves, and whose voice was the sound of the waves.

If the average Manx child born a hundred or more years ago, on whose behalf all the necessary precautions, pagan as well as Christian, had been taken, survived through infancy and escaped abduction into fairyland, it grew up into rather a hard world, experienced poverty and sometimes hunger and became acquainted at a very early age with hard work. The houses in which many such children were born and brought up have disappeared from the lowland fields, and on the hills their fallen stones are known only to wandering mountain sheep. For many their early years were spent playing and working and running about in the fields of a croft or farm, and occasionally, when home concerns permitted, walking miles to get the little schooling that was available.

This kind of childhood known to Manx children for

centuries has ceased to exist and is become like a lost dream.
Something of its background is reflected in the folksongs of
childhood, of which there are not very many. There is one that
was sung as a lullaby, *Ushag Veg Ruy*, Little Red Bird.

> *Ushag Veg Ruy ny moaney dhoo,*
> *C'raad chaddil oo riyr 'syn oie?*
> Little Red Bird of the dark moaney,
> Where did you sleep last night?

The question is repeated in every other verse and in reply
the little bird mentions all its cold sleeping places in turn, the
top of the bush, the tip of the briar, the lath of the house-roof,
As ugh! my chadley cha treih (And O! what a miserable sleep). It
can be imagined how eagerly the child would wait for the last
verse, if it wasn't asleep, and for the night when the bird slept
'between two leaves, like a child between two blankets',

> *Chaddil mish riyr eddyr daa guillag,*
> *Myr ynnagh yn oikan eddyr daa lhuishag,*
> *As O! my chadley cha kiune!*
> And O how peaceful my sleep!

Folksong experts have declared *Ushag Veg Ruy* to be a courting
song disguised, which may be so, but from the rocking rhythm
of both words and tune, it was clearly intended to be used to
lull a child to sleep.

A Manx-speaking mother had other rhymes about birds to
repeat to her children. The language with its soft vowels and
liquid consonants lent itself to the imitation of birdsong. The
best known example is a Manx version of the song of the
Lhondoo, the blackbird that seems to have been particularly
vocal in Gaelic, and the *Ushag-Reaisht*, the mountain plover,
and it relates to a dispute between the pair of them that was
never settled:

> *Lhondoo, lhondoo, vel oo cheet, vel oo cheet?*
> Blackbird, are you coming?
> *Ghiall oo dy darragh oo reesht,*
> You promised you would come again,
> *Skee fieau, skee fieau,*

Tired waiting, tired waiting:
Cha jig dy bragh, Cha jig dy bragh!
I'll never come, I'll never come!
T'eh feer feayr, t'eh feer feayr
It's very cold, very cold!

The child who heard it had no idea how far-travelled was the story of the blackbird of the mountains that changed places with the plover, and found life so much to its liking in the lowlands that it refused to go back to its old haunts among the hills. It is a legend that probably had its origin in Norse mythology, the story of the marriage of Njord and Skadi.

Though children often listened to talk about the fairies, they were not told 'fairy tales' simply for their amusement; they were far too serious a matter for that. They grew up into this other world of their elders, learned how to avoid its perils and earn its rewards and then inhabited it at will. It almost seems as if the supernatural world provided an escape from the pressures and harassments of everyday life. The fairy and other beliefs may have been the last vestiges of an older religious creed, but it was one whose priests and officials had long since vanished, and though the faith itself exercised its own compulsion on its believers, there was a freedom in its demands and in their response to it that was lacking in the obligations and restrictions the real world imposed on them: if, as has sometimes been said, the people were slaves to superstition, it was a bondage they willingly endured.

It was far otherwise with the discipline of the church which bore down upon them all their lives, literally from the cradle to the grave and on all the occasions in between. Private life and personal relationships were constantly under the inquisitorial eye of the Spiritual Courts and their informers, who reported irregularities of conduct and 'presented' offenders for breaches of the Canon law. The impression gained from a cursory reading of Church court records is of a people daily engaged in committing every sin short of murder – adultery, illegitimacy, slander, cursing, sabbath-breaking, tale-bearing and many others. It has been said that 'if the ancient discipline of the church was lost elsewhere, it might be found in all its purity in the Isle of Man.' It could certainly have been found in all its severity. People lived their entire lives under threat of the humiliation of standing at the church door and the market cross in the penitent's sheet, of imprisonment in the dungeons of Peel Castle, and of excommunication. In 1716 a man convicted of adultery and in spite of excommunication still un-reformed, was sentenced 'to stand duely in penitential habit at the parish church door every Lord's day for three years'.

Many of those sentenced were no doubt genuine offenders, but some were mental defectives who could not have been held responsible for their actions. There was the notorious case of Katherine Kinrade in 1713, a woman with three illegitimate children, for whom was decreed a punishment specially designed for women of her kind, of being dragged in the sea by a boat, 'because she still continues to stroll about the country and lead a most vicious and scandalous life'. This sentence was passed on her a second time, for 'after imprisonment, penance and dragging in the sea, continuing still remorseless' and notwithstanding her 'defect of understanding', she was again 'ordered to be twenty-one days close imprison'd and (as soon as the weather permits) dragged in the sea again after a boat, and also perform penance in all the churches of this Island'. It was not only the weather that sometimes prevented this kind of sentence from being carried out; the boatmen objected, refusing to provide boats and rowers, and had to be coerced into it by the military.

Yet the church's strict code was only a thing of its time and must once have sanctioned the custom of 'handfasting', by which a couple might live together for a trial period of a year without marriage. A Kirk Arbory couple whose experiment in matrimony had exceeded the time limit were presented in 1641, having been 'handfasted this whole year and more and doth not marry'.

It is surprising to find under such a rigorous system a courtship custom in existence in the Island which permitted a young man visiting a girl's house to stay after the older people had gone to bed and sit with the daughter until late at night or even until daylight. That this was once customary is evident from Manx folksongs of courtship, but whether the church frowned on it or condoned it is uncertain. Far from enjoying this privilege the young men seem to have regarded the whole business of courtship as something of a penance and to have pursued it with reluctance. *Sooreying*, courting, was done at night after the long day's work, and from the evidence of the folksongs, in winter; perhaps in summer there was no leisure for it.

> With courting in the winter I'd seldom be in bed,
>   But walking in the darkness, scarce seeing the road home.
> My feet also would be wet, and draggled o'er with mire ...
>   Water pouring from my hair, and my teeth chattering.

When he had made the journey in the winter weather he had still to gain admittance, and cold and sodden as he was, he would be kept waiting outside:

> The skin off my knuckles, with tapping the glass outside ...
> Saying, 'My love, my comfort, now do you let me in,
> Could I have only one hour of your company tonight?'

But he was told:

> 'Get away from the window, get away I tell thee,
> For I will not let you in, I know better than that'.

Even when he was inside the house his mind was uneasy;

> I'd be guilty and quake, sitting by the fire,
> E'en at the soot playing behind the gird-iron ...
> Fearing lest there should come some tale-bearer in.

There was the not inconsiderable difficulty of keeping up the conversation:

> When there shall have arrived a little bit of day
> For words I would be spent, I'd have nought to say.

His only reason for relating his miserable tale is that others may benefit from his experience:

> That they may take warning and from courting flee.
> 'Twere better to be lacking a wife all my life,
> Than be bothered and driven and worried like this.

Young women in the folksongs took a much more hopeful view:

'When shall I be wed, mother, the time is very long,
To get myself a helper and defender night and day;
For such a faithful partner would be suitable to my state
For I still have a craving when I am young and gay.'

Her mother's reply is disillusioning, 'Girl, do not go to marry', and she reels off a recital of the ills her daughter might expect if she did – fading beauty, a scolding husband, crying children, sharp words and anger.

There are a few folk songs in Manx which have nothing to do with the mechanics of courtship, but are purely love songs and of a particularly despairing kind. So different are they in sentiment and expression that they scarcely seem to belong to the same tradition as the songs giving practical advice on the folly of courting rich farmers' daughters, and the desirability or otherwise of marrying for the sake of a large dowry. The theme is as melancholy as in the songs of winter courtship; the plaint of the deceived and deserted lover, not of his cold feet and chattering teeth, but of the grief and hopelessness of his heart:

My heart is laden with grief and my mind with sorrow,
My house is bereft of peace and sleep has deserted by bed;
If I'll not get my love to stay with me,
Then I must die without her,

a simple and moving note not often heard in Manx folksong, and its effect is not altogether lost in translation:

The walnut tree that has never spoken,
Other witnesses had I none,
Now my love has proved false to me,
And I am left in grief, alone.

O that the great sea would dry up
And make a way that I might go through;
The snows of Greenland will grow red like roses
Before I can forget my love.

There was formerly a curious adjunct to a Manx court-ship, a friend of the would-be bridegroom who acted as his ambassador or advocate to the girl's parents, and on whom he depended to plead his cause. His name in Manx, *dooinney-moyllee*, literally a 'praising-man', conveys the nature of his role and his duties exactly. He was a go-between, a spokesman who presented his friend in as favourable a light as possible to the girl and her parents, and saw to the business side of the bargain, touching particularly on the important matter of the dowry to be provided, which could make or break the agreement: an observer of the early eighteenth century remarked that 'twenty pounds is a good portion for a mountaineer's daughter, and they are so exact in the marriage bargain, that I have known many who have called themselves hot lovers, break off for the sake of a sow or a pig being refused in the articles'. The dowry sometimes consisted of a gift of land, and farms became so much divided up by the habit of giving a field or part of one as a marriage portion when a girl married, that in some cases they almost ceased to be workable. It may have been because of this fragmentation of family property that the seven bitter curses were laid on Mylecharane of Ballaugh, who was said to have been the first man to give dowry to women.'

On the whole women did reasonably well out of the marriage bargain. Though in the sixteenth century the law stated that, if a man forfeited his goods to the Lord of Man by felony, 'his Wife shall not forfeit her part of the Goods, because the Woman is but subject and obedient to the Man', she seems in fact to have had something approaching equality. An eldest daughter for instance could inherit property where there was no eldest son. By customary law a wife was entitled to half of the goods on her husband's death, and some women apparently laid claim to this half during their husband's lifetime, and disposed of it by will to 'their own kindred in seclusion of their husband's rights', with the result that 'a Man in flourishing easy circumstances, by the Accident of his Wife's Death is utterly ruined'. Women must have been free to do this for a very considerable time, as the law made no attempt to do anything about it until quite late in the eighteenth century.

According to tradition it was only the women of the south side of the Island who were entitled to a half of their husband's goods; those from the north were entitled only to a third. At the battle of Santwat in 1098 the two sides of the Island fought against each other under the chieftains Ottar and Macmarus, and the southside women seeing their men getting the worst of it, descended on the enemy armed with aprons full of stones and succeeded in turning the tide of battle, and so earned for themselves the right to the larger share.

There used to be a saying in the Island, 'No herring, no Wedding'. For many people there was almost complete economic dependence on the herring fishing, and it has been noted that in the parish registers there was direct correspondence each year between the number of marriages recorded and the success or failure of the herring season.

A Manx wedding is one of the traditional social occasions of which the memory has not been allowed to die in the Island. Life is not now always recognisably Manx, far from it, but from time to time there is an upsurge of insular sentiment and it is decided to hold some 'Manx' event: a Manx Tea, a Manx Evening, a *Mheillea,* which is a Manx Harvest Supper, or a Manx Wedding, the most popular of all because it is the most spectacular. Let any village or parish announce a revival of the Manx Wedding, and people will flock there in hundreds. Its chief attraction is the wedding procession in which almost everyone can take part: headed by the bride riding on horseback with her father to the church, then the bridesmaids and groomsmen following two by two, and those not occupying the chief roles, joining in as wedding guests. Apart from the absence of horses and carriages and carts, of which at a real wedding there might once have been fifty or sixty, and the wedding finery which is mostly late Victorian, the scene is much as at an early nineteenth-century wedding, a walking wedding perhaps, when anyone who was met by the wedding party on the way to church had to join in the procession and go along with it until the bridegroom gave them leave to go on their way. The fiddler is there to play for them, as no wedding could be held without him; in the old days there would be two of them:

I remember fiddlers going to weddings. I have been at a wedding myself and the fiddlers going with us to the church and back, and the young men and girls dancing at intervals along the road. There would be four of five dozen young people at the wedding when I was young, walking in pairs... It was a custom for the young men to run a race when returning from the church, the first that reached the house broke the wedding cake into small pieces, and scattered them out of a plate over the head of the bride as she entered, which was thought to increase the dreaming charm.

At an eighteenth-century wedding the 'bride-men' carried osier wands in their hands 'as a mark of their superiority', and before entering the church, the wedding procession walked three times round it. The feast provided after the ceremony was of the proportions of a mediaeval banquet, and in great contrast to the frugal fare of every day: 'I have seen a dozen capons in one platter, and six or eight fat geese in another; sheep and hogs roasted whole and oxen divided but into quarters.'

There are one or two old wedding customs that are kept up or occasionally revived today. As the bride and bridegroom come out of church children will sometimes stretch a rope across the road and hold them up until they have paid their 'footing', which the bridegroom does by throwing them some money to be scrambled for. Young men have been known to revive the old custom of blowing horns outside the home of a girl of their acquaintance the night before she is to be married. In the past this was done to frighten away evil spirits; what the intention is today is hard to say, merely perhaps as a reminder of old times, and because it provides an excuse for making a hideous, but, considering the occasion, a permissible din. Guns are no longer fired on the wedding day to dispel malevolent spirits, but a hundred years ago at some weddings 'they would be firing them all the way to church'.

For the majority of people marriage was 'until death us do part'. Divorce and separation were not lightly regarded nor much sought after, though the church that married a couple would on rare occasions and when circumstances justified, divorce them.

For the ill-usage of a wife by her husband a kind of rough justice was meted out publicly, which was known as 'putting a man on the *stang*'. The male members of the community who disapproved of such a man's behaviour would take a gate off its hinges, lay the offender on it and carry him to his own house, beating him with sticks, mocking him and calling him names all the way, and there deliver him to his wife. The *stang* was literally a pole on which the victim rode, but a gate had the advantage of requiring more men to carry it and so enabled a larger number to express their disapproval.

Changed circumstances and the introduction of new ways of living that might have been expected to destroy the old beliefs, sometimes gave them fresh impetus and set them off in a new direction. This was particularly the case, and not surprisingly, with the superstitions surrounding death and burial, for they will probably be the very last to disappear, if they ever do.

People were very much concerned in the past with the signs of death, and discovered them in things that in themselves were quite ordinary, the behaviour of children, animals and birds, but it was the place or time or the way they were heard and seen and done that made them unnatural and exceptional and recognisable as a 'sign'. To dream of something quite pleasant like dressing a child was one of them as 'dreams went by opposites'. Children at play who started marching up and down were quite unknown to themselves giving warning of a coming death to those who saw them: 'I have seen the old people watching the children playing on the green, sometimes they would be singing and marching about, carrying a stool or a stick on their shoulders or something of that sort, the old folk said it was a sign of a funeral.' A swarm of bees in summer was a common enough sight, but a swarm disappearing down the chimney of a house must surely have been an infrequent occurrence and meant a death in the family living there. There was one house where this was seen to happen three times in three years: 'It's a sign of death man, yes it is, for there was three swarms came them three years one after another into the chimley of the house, an' I lost three, one after the other, a big lump of a boy and two gels, it was a terrible loss.'

Other death signs were sparks from the fire seen coming out through the chimney, a bird flying against the window or into a room, a dog howling or a cock crowing at night, provided that if its feet were cold, this needed investigation, as a night-crowing cock with warm feet foretold a wedding!

Many signs of death and of a forthcoming funeral were not general warnings of this kind, but were directly related to the funeral of someone about to die. Poorer people in the Island were often buried without a coffin and their funeral issued from a small single storey house where the corpse had lain for the *aaght-oie*, or night of lodging, the wake-in one or other of its ground-floor rooms; except for a cock-loft; the old Manx house had no 'upstairs'. But from the nineteenth century a new and rather sensational kind of folklore began to develop, which is probably to be attributed to the more general use of coffins for burial and to the fact that more people began to live in houses with two storeys and a staircase between them. Though these innovations gave added scope for and effect to the stories that began to be told of death and funeral signs, the stories were only a more elaborate version of the much older beliefs already in circulation.

The phenomenon of the ghostly funeral was well enough known in Waldron's day:

> The natives of the Island tell you also that before any person dies the procession of the funeral is acted by a sort of beings which for that end render themselves invisible. I know several that have offered to make oath that as they have been passing the road, one of these funerals has come behind them, and even laid the bier on his shoulders, as though to assist the bearers. One person, who assured me he had been served so, told me that the flesh of his shoulder had been very much bruised, and was black for many weeks after.

In days gone by when a number of Manx people, especially country people met together, and the older ones among them started reminiscing, the talk would turn sooner or later to recollections of supernatural happenings and 'signs'. Someone would begin to tell how one day as he was going past a particular church or chapel, he thought he heard the sound of voices singing inside; he could even recognise the tune although it was a week day and he knew the place was empty. Only a few days afterwards he went there to a funeral service, and the very same hymn was sung that he had heard when he was passing in the road. This would remind someone else of an experience he had had, when he was going along the road to the churchyard and had suddenly felt as if he was being pushed aside and jostled by a throng of people in the road, although he could see nobody. Then some days later he remembered the strange sensation he had felt of being in the middle of a crowd of people, when he was walking along the road again to the churchyard, this time in the midst of a real crowd going to a funeral. Stories of these ghostly meetings near churchyards were still being told in the early part of this century and it is quite possible that there are people about who could still tell them.

When coffins eventually came into general use in the Island they must have made a deep impression on people's minds when brought to a house where someone had died; and worked on their imagination, for the superstitions of death and burial began to centre round them. What they did chiefly was to contribute a whole new range of sound effects to the hitherto fairly quiet solemnities of the old style of Manx burial ceremony when the corpse was simply laid on an open bier to be carried to the graveyard. The pre-hearing of the singing that will be heard at a funeral is hundreds of years old; it was reported as a feature of the phantom funeral in the eighteenth century, 'they sing psalms in the same manner as those do who accompany the corpse of a dead friend'. The latter-day folklore of coffin burial is only a further extension and development of this old belief, with the sounds that will be made when a coffin is brought into a house substituted for the singing. A recital of these macabre premonitory noises is as eerie as any ghost story, and the person claiming to have heard them can by their own conviction evoke them again in the telling: quiet footsteps on the stairs, bumping noises as the narrow staircase is negotiated, the sound of something being dragged along the bedroom floor, then later, careful, more laboured footsteps coming down again. There could even be an advance hearing of the undertaker's conversation or of the voices of people who called to sympathise – the whole experience and circumstances of the death and funeral heard in advance, but only in retrospect recognised for what they were.

When a death occurred the immortal spirit manifested itself as a light, and at the moment of a person's death a light would be seen coming out of the door of the house and moving towards the churchyard. Baring-Gould mentions the flames that in Icelandic Saga 'flicker and wave above the tumuli covering dead warriors'. This fire was an indication of the continuing life of those within the mound. There was an Irish sea captain whose ship was wrecked off the coast of the Isle of Man, and though he escaped himself, he lost thirteen men of his crew. When he came ashore he was astonished to find that the people already knew how many of his men had been drowned; on the night of the shipwreck they had seen thirteen lights moving in from the sea towards Rushen churchyard.

When the dead were being prepared for burial, it was essential that they should not be restricted in any way; the grave clothes must be loose, all knots left untied to allow the spirit to go free, and so that there should be nothing to hinder or impede it at the resurrection. To neglect this loosening was to fetter the departing soul. There is one known case of a ghost that was found in this predicament after it had left this world.

A man met a ghos'; there were knots at the ghos' and he wanted the knots loosened. The man who spoke to him could not get rid of him or away, and he tried to loose it but it became tighter, and he put his hand in his pocket to pull out his knife to cut it ... but it dropped on the ground and he had to loose it with his teeth. After that he was laid up for a long time.

The spirits of the dead were known to be of a restless nature which was why people feared them. The pagan tried to keep them in their graves with gift offerings, but there were other methods resorted to. 'A blacksmith was asked to put a cross of iron on a grave to keep the spirit from coming out, but it happened the ghos' was out and could not get in, and he was angry and he shouted, *"Trog shoh"* ("Lift this") and the man has never done any good afterwards.'

The dead were never left alone or in the dark. Candles were kept burning in the room where they lay, and the body was waked. There was nothing private in any of the great occasions of life in days gone by. Whether one was being born or dying, marrying or being buried, it was a public matter and friends and relations gathered round. The waking of a corpse was a custom that continued into the nineteenth century, when people came to the house to eat and drink and smoke pipes of tobacco. It may have been smuggled tobacco at one time, but quite sizable amounts figure in some funeral expense accounts for ale and tobacco. There was music and singing throughout the *aaght-oie,* the night of lodging of the dead, and an indispensable member of this as of all such social gatherings was the fiddler 'who was valued as much as the parson' and got his fee (known for rather obscure but explicable reasons as the *Unnysup*) for playing and accompanying the singing. It is recalled that the music at a wake was 'very mournful' but no example of it has survived. Some of the old Manx carval tunes usually associated with a special church service on Christmas Eve might well have been sung at a wake. *O Colb ec Shee,* for instance, 'O body at rest', seems in the appropriate category, a slow and solemn tune like the voice of the grave itself.

Until quite recently at funerals a hymn was sung at the house door before the coffin was taken away. Formerly a funeral dirge, a *Bardoon,* was sung as the funeral cortege went along the road, the parish clerk going in front and lining the hymn out verse by verse, and the people taking it up in response. Other musical accompaniments of funerals, passing bells, bells for the dead in the church, 'carrying bells and banners before the dead' were slowly relinquished after the Reformation.

There was nothing in the solemnities of a funeral capable of suppressing the natural tendency towards conviviality. It has been rightly said that, except in the case of the immediately bereaved and their close relatives, a funeral tended to be regarded more as a social gathering to which everyone went, though with the very sincere intention of honouring the dead and 'seeing them home' in a fitting manner. Within the last twenty years or so an old Manx woman apologising for arriving late at her friend's house made the excuse that she had been 'enjoying herself'. She had in fact been to a funeral. In the case of the wake and the funeral, the same degree of hospitality was expected by and extended to all who came, as on the occasions of rejoicing dealt with in this chapter; plenty of food and home-brewed Manx *jough,* or ale, was provided. There was the same rounding off of the occasion when righteous moral indignation was being expressed by putting someone on the stang, for wife-beating, or perhaps even for drunkenness. When the proceedings were concluded and the offender punished to everyone's satisfaction, 'they all went to the tavern to get ale over it'.

6 The Folk and the Barons

THE FIRST STANLEYS found their Island kingdom rather less than they had hoped for economically, and their dissatisfaction and frustration were aggravated rather than assuaged by the clear prospect it afforded from its highest mountains of the neighbouring countries across the Irish sea. 'Five kingdoms at a glance' is the boasted view from the Island's highest hills, and today, someone catching a glimpse of the distant coast of England, Ireland, or Scotland, or, more exceptionally and ominously, the faint shadow on the southern horizon that is Wales, while marvelling at the clarity of the atmosphere, would tend to consider the prospect in terms of forthcoming spells of fine, or more likely stormy weather ahead. To the seventh Earl of Derby however, the sight was no mere weather sign. 'When I go on the Mount you call Baroull, and but turning me round can see England, Scotland, Ireland and Wales, I think shame so fruitlessly to see so many kingdoms at once (which no place I think in any nation that we know under heaven can afford such a prospect) and have so little profit by them.' Even within the Island their sway did not extend throughout its entire length and breadth, and the 'profit' of its lands was not all theirs. Since the time of the Norse kings of Man, certain grants of land had been made to various religious houses and orders outside the Island's bounds, whose heads along with the Manx Bishop, the Abbot of Rushen Abbey and the Prioress of Douglas were barons of the Island, eight in number altogether. The foreign barons, the Abbot of Furness, the Abbots of Bangor and Sabhal in Ireland, the Prior of St Bees in Cumberland, and the Prior of Whithorn in Galloway, had each a territorial footing in the Island, holding their lands independently and receiving the rents, dues and services of the tenants on their farms, and in some cases having their own Manorial Court.

These insular and foreign landlords holding extensive tracts of land in the Island, not only represented the great and still-increasing power of the church, but their presence had considerable repercussions on the personal lives of those who for some centuries lived as tenants on their domains. The Cistercian monks of Rushen Abbey, possessors of much farmland were probably to a large extent beneficent landlords, and almost certainly encouraged the development of agriculture here. One writer even goes so far as to say that the monks left their mark on the Manx character, inculcating those qualities of caution, piety, frugality and industry that are supposed or were once supposed to characterise Manx country and farming people: hundreds of years later a similar claim was made for Methodism. It is highly improbable that any individual, still less a whole people, could ever be converted permanently to such a negatively virtuous state. Certainly the Manxman is noted for his caution, and circumstances often compelled him to be frugal, but a study of insular records and of folklore tends to suggest that these virtues were sometimes only an acquired veneer overlying the much more complex variety of qualities, just as much if not more rooted in the past, which go to make the Manx character.

The tenure of land by ecclesiastical authorities, while

sometimes conferring benefits, also imposed obligations, and this fact has been perpetuated in some of the more interesting and unusual farm names. In the parish of Maughold the treen of Ballaterson was held on a freehold tenancy in return for the safe keeping of the pastoral staff of St Maughold, the patron saint of the parish. The name means the farm of the staff or crozier. With the exception of St Patrick, more wonders are told of St Maughold in Manx legend than of any other saint, and they did not cease with his death. The Chronicle of Man relates that when Somerled invaded the Island in 1158, Gilcolm one of his followers planned to drive off the cattle that were grazing outside the walls of the monastery at Maughold for the use of the army. The people supplicated the long-dead saint, and he appeared to Gilcolm in a dream bearing his staff, and with it pierced him to the heart. Awaking from his dream in agony, Gilcolm sent his followers to the church to bring the staff and priests and clerks who would intercede for him with St Maughold, but when they came, they prayed to the saint, not to remove Gilcolm's affliction, but to prolong it until he died. 'Thus shall others by seeing and hearing thy punishment, learn to pay due respect to hallowed ground.' It has been suggested that the ancient staff of St Maughold may have been handed down from the earliest days of the Celtic monastery at Maughold, and was perhaps one of the Three Reliques of Man, otherwise unidentified, that before the Reformation were borne at the Tynwald by 'Three Clearkes in their Surplisses'.

There were stafflands also of St Patrick, but it is only of the staff of St Maughold that history has very much to say, though the name Ballaterson is found in some other parishes on farms adjoining ecclesiastical land, but if any of them had similar legends attached to them or any tradition of service to account for the name, they have been forgotten. Certain church lands which in the records are called 'particles' were allocated to the church for educational purposes, 'for the support of poor scholars', possibly for the benefit of those destined for the priesthood. There were some occasions when the poor scholars were deprived of their rights, and the revenues of the particles were seized by greedy churchmen and Lords of Man, and 'dealt into other uses'. Learning for the bulk of the people was always hard come by, and in these early days such education as was available was confined within the walls of the religious houses, in Rushen Abbey where the monks wrote their Chronicle of the Island's history and possibly in similar establishments that have left no record. This was to be the case for centuries to come, the church having the sole responsibility for the enlightenment and instruction of their people, while at the same time enriching themselves on the tithes and duties levied on the produce of their land, and on their personal property. The church's grip on the people was of long standing, for since the beginning of the thirteenth century their obligations to their spiritual masters had been clearly defined in written law. Yet the people themselves were kept in ignorance. Even after the Reformation it was a frequent complaint that the church service was unintelligible to them because it was read in English, not in the Gaelic which was the only language most of them understood. 'There is no Manx sermon in our church, not so much as one in the year, for the edification of the people, who understand no other language, the want thereof is a great grief to the people.' This was the complaint of Kirk Maughold parishioners in 1642, and a century later, after the Bible had been translated into Manx, an old woman hearing a passage read was moved to exclaim, 'Until now we have sat in Darkness'.

Burdened with heavy tithe obligations, spiritually and intellectually deprived, Manx attitudes to wealth and learning over the years had had plenty of time to mature. The language contains a proverb which shows how readily the bulk of the people accepted the idea that any higher standard of enlightenment for themselves was, if not wholly unattainable, at least a luxury, while for the wealthy it was their natural right and privilege: *'Ta ynsagh coamrey stoamey yn dooinney berchagh, as t'eh berchys yn dooinney boght'* ('Learning is the fine raiment of the rich man, and it is the riches of the poor'). It reflects an attitude that has not died out even yet in some people's minds, one that influences their reaction to others' attainment in life. Of someone who has achieved success or distinction they are apt to say in sheer disbelief, 'I knew his grandfather'. It is based less on envy than on this feeling of incredulity: the people they knew and grew up with, though claiming the right to the 'fine raiment', can never wear it convincingly, the known and familiar can never become the great and distinguished. The corollary of this is probably that greatness like beauty is in the eye of the beholder, and a reputation for it is best maintained at a distance.

When the Stanleys first came to the Island in the fifteenth century the church had a greater hold over the people and was in a stronger position than the civil power. The ecclesiastical barons in whom this power was vested seem on occasion to have been as recalcitrant and arrogant as any of the famed bad barons of English history, neglecting to do fealty to the Lord of Man from whom they held their lands. But the second Sir John Stanley, himself no weakling, 'a man who gave neither toleration nor termon (sanctuary) to ecclesiastics, laymen or literary men', set about curbing their power. He allowed them forty days in which to come and do fealty to him, but if within that time they failed to come they were to forfeit their possessions.

At the beginning of the Stanley period, the state was weak, the Tynwald, the Manx parliament had fallen into disuse, and its procedure had to be deemed afresh to the new Lord of Man by the Deemsters and other experienced and worthy men, who calling to remembrance 'the Constitution of Old Time', instructed him:

> ... how you should be governed on your Tynwald Dayes ... You shall come hither in your Royal Array as a King ought to do ... and upon the Hill of Tynwald sitt in a Chaire, covered with a Royal Cloath and Cushions, and your Visage unto the East, and your Sword before you, holden with the Point upward; your Barrons in the third degree sitting beside you, and your beneficed Men and your Deemsters before you sitting; and your Clearkes, your Knights, Esquires and Yeomen, about you in the third degree; and the worthiest Men in your Land to be called in before your Deemsters, if you will ask any Thing of Them ... and the Commons to stand without the Circle of the Hill, with three Clearkes in their Surplisses ... and all the Coroners of Man, and their Yards in their Hands, with their Weapons upon them, either Sword or Axe ...

– a spectacle remembered 'from King Orryes Dayes' and handed down to these Manx elders by their predecessors, and one which shorn of some of its more military aspects, certainly with fewer 'Barrons in the third degree' is still witnessed by thousands of people, many of them holiday-makers who swell the numbers of the 'Commons standing without the Circle of the Hill' at the Tynwald ceremony – the open-air meeting of the Manx parliament which is held each year on 5 July at the height of the tourist season.

The reinstatement of the Tynwald in 1422 after a lapse of many years was an event of great importance for the Manx nation. Today the laws are promulgated from the hill, and until only fairly recently were not effective until they had been proclaimed to the assembled people in Manx as well as in English, and at this historic gathering in the early fifteenth century the Manx constitution was defined, its ceremony and procedure outlined and its laws written down for the first time; laws that were 'rattifyed, approved and confirmed' not ony by the 'Barrons, Deemsters and Officers', but also by the 'Tennants, Inhabitants and Commons of the Land of Man', as they have been each year since then.

Manx historians have modestly suggested that in the adoption of certain measures at the resumed Tynwald, the Manx people showed themselves to be politically in advance of some of their neighbours across the sea. Trial by 'prowess' or combat was replaced by trial by jury, and the Barons' right of Sanctuary was abolished. This blow struck at the Barons of the Manx church, the Abbots, the Priors and the Bishop, depriving them of their right of Sanctuary several years before it was abolished in England was certainly significant – a deliberate attempt on the part of Sir John Stanley to crush the power of the church, a first move in the long-drawn-out struggle between the two powers that was to continue through much of the period of Stanley rule. The Lord's war against the Barons was carried into the enemies' territory, when his representative, pressing home the advantage already gained, held a Court within the Bishop's own boundaries, on the Hill of Reneurling in Kirk Michael, where the Bishop and other Barons, who hitherto had failed to come and do obedience to the new ruler, were bidden to do so.

Some commentators have put an exaggerated interpretation on these undeniably decisive events in Manx history. Folklore is not – or should not be – a narrow and exclusive study of one section of the community. The mental attitudes of the scholarly are sometimes just as revealing and as worthy of investigation as the ways of the folk which they seek to interpret. They merely demonstrate the workings of a different set of superstitions. In the case of a nineteenth-century editor of a compilation of the legislation of the Stanleys, it was religious bias which made him attribute some very questionable motives to the people of the Island during the events of the fifteenth century, and cast the Island itself in a mighty, and mightily exaggerated role. His assertion that Sir John Stanley, in setting himself to curb the power of the church, was 'the Great Manx Hammer of the Papacy; it was his regal power that by constitutional means and written law put down the Papal power in the Isle,' is possibly true as far as the Island is concerned, but this was only his moderate beginning, and thereafter his pen and his prejudices run away with his judgement, if he had any. His style is highly inflated, and he is at his most dramatic over the barons' fall from power: 'At one blow he levelled to the dust all the baronial sanctuaries ... It was the first collision between the King of Lilliput and the Giant of Rome.' He wrote like a Great Hammer himself, and is never moderate, and he could be quoted endlessly. On the scene at Reneurling he dwells lovingly, gloating over the humiliation of the Bishop who was compelled to do fealty to the Lord in the presence of the people: 'On Reneurling Hill in 1422 we find a miniature picture of the Protestant British Empire – Kings, Barons, Commons are there – and the Pope's representative crouching at their feet. It is the embryo of the mighty Protestant Empire. The primary germ cell and the first spark of life commenced at the heart of the British Isles.' He goes on to describe the orders and degrees of precedence on the hill at Tynwald, and observes with intense satisfaction the changed status of the barons, at whom he never ceases to nag and worry throughout his whole diatribe, and who, though still occupying chief places, were there 'only in their capacity as the Peers of the King Stanley, not as Peers of the Papacy'; he rejoices to find that to the representative of the Papacy 'the Three Relics of Man and the Three Clearkes bearing them in their Surplisses, the last and lowest place is assigned'. He saw the Island at this moment as the centre of a world struggle: 'The Battle was great as the field was small. Gigantic principles contended in a Lilliputian Sphere'. It was as David confronting Goliath. 'I was born free, said the apostle Paul and the Island's constitution was born free of Popery and an enemy of the Papacy.' Then comes the grand climax – 'From Spanish

Head' – an unfortunate choice of name in the circumstances –
'it frowned defiance to slavery, Spain and the Pope.' So he
rants on for nearly a hundred pages, making exaggerated
claims and far-fetched comparisons on almost every one. His
tirade is best explained by disclosing his identity as the Rev.
William Mackenzie, a member of the Free Presbytery of
Edinburgh, who was editing this publication in 1850, when
the Roman Catholic church was seeking to re-establish itself
in England, and anti-Catholic feeling was running high in the
Island as elsewhere in the country. At a public meeting in
Douglas presided over by 'respectable gentlemen of Douglas
and its neighbourhood', protests to 'Papal aggression' had the
true Mackenzie ring; 'Protestants of every denomination from
the Calf of Man to the Point of Ayr, will unite with their
English brethren to repel the encroachments of Popery.' Even
the miners of Laxey Glen, backed by the Chaplain and the
schoolmaster, petitioned the Queen to stand firm on the issue
on their behalf. Over the next decade Protestant opposition
continued to express itself in various ways, from the singing of
doggerel in the streets, 'We'll get a rope, and hang the Pope',
to the emergence of Protestant Protection and Protestant
Young Men's Societies and even of one or two Orange Lodges.

It would require a less prejudiced historian than Mackenzie
to make a fair assessment of events in the Island in the
fifteenth century, but folklore can reply to some of his
allegations, both in the legends that grew out of the historical
situation, and in what is remembered and handed down of the
people's reaction to those representatives of the Old Religion,
and of the pre-Reformation conditions of life generally, when
the Barons of the Roman church were the landlords and
employers of a good many of the people, and under the
Papacy, the spiritual masters of them all.

Reformation came slowly in the Isle of Man, and the old
Catholic observances lingered on. People continued to carry
bells and banners before the dead, until the state, not the
church, legislated against it. Praying for the dead 'and other
reliques of popish superstition' existed as late as 1688. Bishop
Levinz who complained of this said that 'as soon as any person
is interred all the persons present fall down upon their knees
and say their prayers at the grave, of which ask them the
reason, they can tell you no other but that their fathers did so
before them'. There was a tradition that Irish priests used to

visit the Island secretly to celebrate Mass in some of the old keeills in the Island; this is told of Lhag ny Keeilley in Patrick and the chapel at Kerrookeil also has late Catholic associations. Waldron speaks of 'Popish priests' being sent over to the Island to 'exercise their function' in private houses. The old Catholic chapel at the south end of Douglas was pulled down, and a house was built on the site.

> The woman who occupied this house with her husband, and who often used to sit up waiting for him to return till a very late hour, declared that every night when the clock struck twelve she distinctly heard the tramp of many feet entering the room where she sat. Then there was silence, and after a time the sound of feet again. Doubtless this was the arrival of the ancient worshippers at midnight Mass and their departure from it.

The words of some of the old charms – especially blood-stopping charms – show definite Catholic influence. There was the charm to staunch bleeding in horses which translates from the Manx: 'Three Maries went to Rome, the Spirits of the Church stiles, and the Spirits of the houghs, Peter and Paul: one Mary said: may this blood stop as the blood stopped which came out of the wounds of Christ: me to say it and the Son of Mary to fulfil it.' Another was in Latin and must never be used in any other language: if it was translated its efficacy in stopping bleeding would be lost for ever.

> *Sanguis mane in te,*
> *Sicut Christus in se;*
> *Sanguis mane in tua vena,*
> *Sicut Christus in sua poena;*
> *Sanguis mane fixus*
> *Sicut erat Christus*
> *Quando fuit crucifixus.*

Tradition has very little to say directly of how the people fared under the monks before the Reformation; it is information that has to be deduced from the evidence available. It is probable that after the Dissolution in 1539 they were worse rather than better off. The charitable institutions or hospitals connected with some of the religious houses, of which there is some record, the Hospital of Ballacgniba or Greeba on the Barony of St Trinian's and Boayl y Spital, the place of the hospital, in Kirk German, and associated by tradition with the Knights of St John of Jerusalem, even if they had survived the plundering attacks of raiders, would have ceased to function with the collapse of the organisations that maintained them.

On many of the quarterland farms in the Island it was always the custom to provide hospitality, food and shelter for the wandering beggars who travelled about the roads, people who got their living by 'going on the houses', as it was called. They were usually otherwise homeless, going about from place to place, relying on people's charity to provide them with a bed and some food, oatmeal or potatoes or a salt herring to put in their *wallad*. The insular law dealt very strictly with them, ordering them to be whipped and sent back to their own parish and maintained there, a law which seems to have been largely disregarded, for they were made welcome; no-one ever turned them away, but accepted them as part of the pattern of life. Some farms, even up to the nineteenth century, had a beggars' house (one or two of them still in existence) a small house with a fireplace, where beds were provided and there was a fire to sit by: on many farms the travellers were allowed to sleep in the barn, first surrendering any matches they might have in their possession. This habit of willing hospitality is possibly one of the social attitudes taught to the people long ago by the religious orders. It is perhaps an indication of the origin of the custom that the farms constituting the grant of land on which the hospital of Ballacgniba was founded were themselves places where the beggars were housed and fed. It has been suggested that the name of one of them, Ballavitchal, comes from the Irish *bally-biatach,* the land held by the keeper of a hostel or hospice for the entertainment of travellers and of the poor. The Irish records mention several varieties of places of this kind, from Da Derga's Hostel of the legends to places of sanctuary for murderers, and hospices for travellers and the poor. 'The Irish missionaries carried this fine custom to the Continent in early ages ... they established *hospitalia* chiefly for the use of pilgrims on their way to Rome', and it is perhaps permissible to suppose that they or their successors may have brought it here.

After the Dissolution, which in the Island took effect only slowly since the edict did not apply to it, the lands and possessions of the ecclesiastical barons were taken possession of by the Lord of Man, or were 'seized to the Queen's use' and some of them came eventually into private hands. As once the title of King had proved attractive to prospective Lords of Man, so when certain of the former church lands became vacant there were ambitious, though misinformed, individuals who were tempted to take possession of them so that they might call themselves Barons. In the west of the Island, the Barony of Bangor and Sabhal, lands previously held by the Abbots of the religious houses of these names in County Down in Ulster, came after some years into the hands of 'a Mr Carrington and one Mr Chew who ... caught with the pompous title of a baron and flattering themselves that the soil and freehold were granted took up the patent for thirty-one years, but coming to the Island found it an empty name'. Such changes in ownership bore hard on the people, for they usually meant that they had become the tenants of greedy and unscrupulous landlords who cared nothing about their welfare, but only for their own profit, and who tried to increase their rents, and even questioned their right of tenure. In 1751 some of the poor tenants of the Barony of Bangor and Sabhal, most of whom had probably never left their homes except in the course of their everyday affairs were presented with an alarming ultimatum. The land they lived on had by this time passed to a John Nicholson of Surrey, yet a third aspirant to the title of Baron, who seemed to have shared the reaction of his predecessors in the property, the disillusioned Carrington and Chew. But, instead of relinquishing it as they had done, he 'commenced a suit of Exchequer of the freehold and inheritance of the Lands of the Barony, serving subpoenas on the tenants and requiring them to attend in London in connection with a suit for possession'. This was an impossible demand to make on such people in those days, for, as was pointed out in a petition on their behalf to the Duke of Athol, by then Lord of Man, they had never before left the Island, knew no English and had no means of meeting the expense of the journey. The matter hung in the balance for twelve long-drawn-out years of litigation, while the tenants waited for their fate to be settled, but it is possible that they imagined themselves to be more insecure than was actually the case.

The old Manx customary law of the tenure of the straw so-called because a tenant quitting his land tendered a straw as token of relinquishment, when the land passed to a new tenant, was far more soundly based than its rather frail-sounding name might suggest, and was to stand firm on this occasion as it had in the past when one of the Derbys tried to turn it into a leasehold tenure. John Nicholson found that he could not set it aside but was 'glad to take the ancient reserved Rents, Boons, etc with which the poor tenants complied, so that their tenure of the straw was never altered'.

A previous grant of the Barony had been made to the Sherburnes of Lancashire and in 1671 Richard Sherburne had also tried to increase the tenants' customary payments. Their response had been to send a petition to the Earl of Derby claiming that under the Abbots of Bangor and Sabhal 'their ancestors had happily and comfortably held their land and had never been burdened with any other imposicion more than the payment of their ancient rents, Boons, duties, customs and services, until now'.

This testimony of satisfaction from the tenants of one of the Baronies rather gives the lie to the Rev Mackenzie's assertion that the people had 'a deep-rooted hatred of Papal rule', which 'was prominent in their history', and directed especially against 'the dumb dogs that could never have enough in Rushen Abbey and German Cathedral': the Manx he maintains 'adopted the Anglican church because they were not compelled. The Liturgy that Scotland refused at the point of the bayonet, Man received with love and reverence.' Yet centuries later when many Manx people turned from Anglicanism to Methodism, the reason given in some quarters was their inability to understand and appreciate the beauty of this same liturgy.

It isn't surprising that the few stories remembered about the monks should be about their greed and its consequences; this is the kind of thing that people always remember. Tradition has it that the monks of Rushen Abbey travelling southward along the upland road called after them, the Bayr ny Mannaghyn, the Monks' Road, their horses well-laden with the tithe-grain and other produce their tenants on the northside farms had been compelled to part with, lost the most of it as they crossed over the ford of the flooded river, so had little gain from their long journey. The tale of this would soon travel back to the aggrieved farmers, and the telling of it console them for years to come. It is only one tale, but there may have been many occasions out of which it grew, when by the intervention of Providence the folk had the laugh on the barons. They paid tithe not only on grain, but on the fish they caught, on their livestock, even if they only possessed one or two animals, on their butter and cheese; a time came when they were refused communion if they failed to present their tithes of dairy produce and money offering at Easter, this being possible as until 1643, the payment of the 'milk tithe' was made on the Sabbath day in the church upon the altar.

The tithe war went on, long after the barons were dispossessed of their wealth, and only one remained, the Bishop of the Diocese, who still ranks as one. The Curse of God and sundry other maledictions were frequently called down on the tithe-collectors, and when the avaricious clergy in the early nineteenth century attempted to get payment out of the newly introduced crops of potatoes and turnips, there was rioting and burning. In 1839 the tithe was commuted for a money payment, but the memory of it lived and lives on to this day. 'They would be saying of any poor crop they had, or of some beast that hadn't thrived and was under-sized, that it would do for the church – anything was good enough for that.' The story of the preparation of the tithe corn was often recalled in after years. 'Old —— used to be saying that in his grandfather's time when they were in the harvest at Balla —— they had to put so many sheaves to one side to pay the tithe. So they would be making the bands, and then gathering up the corn out of the swathe with the most thistles and docks in it, then tying it up with some of the good corn on the oustide so the weeds wouldn't be seen so well. They would never give the good sheaves if they could help it.' This was the attitude to their obligations that Bishop Wilson complained of. His tenants in Jurby were in the habit of 'paying their customes in ye worst grain and goods they can get, so that I am forced to return it or flinge it away'. His Kirk Braddan tenants went a shade further : 'some of the tenants having not given bad enough, but have borrowed worse than their own to pay in.'

Folk memory for such grievances as these is long and retentive, but it might seem improbable that the protracted struggle between church and state should be remembered in any way, or the history of the baronies themselves have left any recognizable traces in folklore. It is true that no unappeased and wrathful baron haunts the old baron lands in any immediately recognizable form. The Ree Mooar ny Howe, the Great King of the Hill about whom Kirk Maughold children were warned when they went to mind the sheep on Christian's Barony that was once the property of the Priory of St Bee's, was more likely to have been an ancient ghost out of one of the tumuli on the hill, perhaps even risen from Cashtal yn Ard, the neolithic burial ground close by. The spirits that haunted and brooded over the baronies were of rather a different kind.

It is curious that 'The Barony' should still survive as a farm name as it does in Maughold, and the old name 'Abbeylands' be found even yet in some parishes for the former possessions of Rushen Abbey, persisting in house and place names, Abbey Cottage, Abbey View, Abbey Mill. The Methodists kept it in naming their chapels, Abbeylands Lonan, Abbeylands Onchan. Clearly neither the memory of the monks nor the church they stood for held any threat for the early Wesleyans.

There is a tradition in the south of the Island that can be taken back to a time when the dividing line between the lands of Rushen Abbey and those of the Lord of Man was a matter of life and death. On the road from Douglas to the south there is a bridge over the Santon river at Ballaglonney that no-one with any knowledge of Manx superstition would cross, on foot or driving, without in some way acknowledging the presence of the fairies who live there. All that is required is to raise a hand in salutation and murmur *'Cre'n aght ta shiu?'* ('How are you?'), or some such greeting, and all will be well, but if this courtesy is neglected anything can happen, and usually something quite unpleasant, from a flat tyre to a bad accident. This bridge has in late years become so notorious as a haunt of the fairies that on a fairly recent royal visit, the belief was taken to the absurd length of arranging for small 'fairies' hidden behind the low stone wall of the bridge to rise up at the appropriate moment and greet the royal car, whose occupants, possibly forewarned of this supernatural manifestation, stopped and greeted them. For some time after this happy encounter, officialdom and the press became so besotted with their pet fancy that 'the fairy bridge' especially during the tourist season was hardly ever out of the news. All this in spite of the fact that Ordnance Survey maps show, and from oral sources it is evident, that the 'true' fairy bridge is on an old pack-horse road that crosses a stream farther to the north-east. However, the Santon river may carry fairy and other tradition along a good stretch of its length, for it is not only the boundary between the parishes of Santon and Malew, but also once divided the lands of Rushen Abbey from those of the Lord of Mann. The felon or outlaw, fleeing long ago from retribution to seek sanctuary with the monks, might well, on fording the river and first setting foot on land where the Lord's justice could not reach him, have crossed himself or uttered a prayer of thankfulness for his safety. From this 'a greeting to the fairies' could have been substituted later on, as less complicated in origin than a purely historical explanation, and more in keeping with Manx tradition. For the fairies, as has been seen were creatures of many backgrounds and origins, and the people were ever prone to making these substitutions, replacing pious associations with pagan ones, in spite of the church's constant efforts to reverse the process.

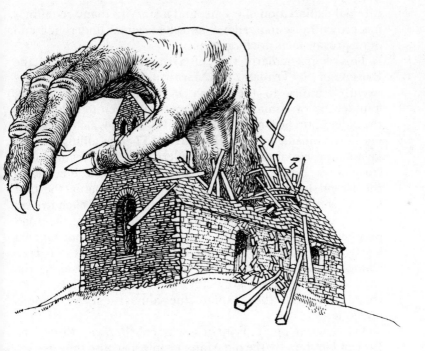

7 The Buggane of St Trinian's

IT MIGHT BE SAID, and with some justification no doubt, that an entirely exaggerated significance could be attributed to the stories and legends that centre round the former baronies. They could have been told of other places in the Island, but because of the strife and dissension inherent in the historical situation, and the fact that the barons of the church represented an intrusive foreign element in the lives of the people, it was inevitable that the folklore that grew up in and around their possessions should reflect this contact with the outside world.

In some instances time and memory have played strange tricks with the historical basis of this kind of tradition, so that it survives in a completely disguised form. Popular preference has almost always been for a supernatural rather than a rational explanation of events, and a story in many re-tellings has grown more marvellous, and the original underlying and often prosaic facts are forgotten.

This is particularly true of a story that belongs to the Barony of St Trinian's in Marown, lands granted in the twelfth century to the Priory of Whithorn in Galloway, founded by St Ninian, whose name was given to only one of the older churches in the Island, St Trinian's, which stands on one of the hillside farms of the Barony. There is almost need of an apology, certainly to Manx readers, for telling yet again the story of the Buggane of St Trinian's. Everyone who comes to the Island hears it sooner or later; it is probably the best known of all Manx fairy stories, a stock yarn of coach drivers who taking their load of summer visitors along the road between Peel and Douglas, and having pointed out Greeba Castle, 'the home of the famous Manx novelist Sir Hall Caine', slow down near a gateway a little further along the road where a roofless grey stone-built church stands in the trees, and tells them about the almost equally famous buggane.

The church of St Trinian's was called *Keeill Brisht,* the Broken Church, by the old Manx people, because they used to say that it was never finished, and whether this was so or not, it has remained roofless to this day. It was not from lack of trying that it has never had a roof, but every time an attempt was made to put it on, a terrible buggane, 'with a head of coarse black hair and eyes like torches', rose out of the ground and brought it crashing down. In a public house along the main road from Douglas to Peel there are still kept a large pair of scissors and a thimble, which, it is claimed, were used by a tailor called Timothy, who when the roof was being put on St Trinian's yet again and was almost finished, sat down one night in the chancel of the church, cross-legged in his customary fashion, determined to make a pair of breeches before the buggane could show himself and set about his evil work. He sat there sewing undisturbed until he had reached the last seam, when with a terrible roar the buggane began to heave himself up from underneath the flagged floor. Having got his head above ground, he caught sight of Timothy sitting there sewing and taking no notice of him, which made him very angry, and as he hauled his huge body out of the hole, he began to utter threats: 'Do thou see my big head?' he roared,

'Do thou see my long arms and my sharp claws?', shaking his fist in the tailor's face. To every threat Timothy, though he was frightened out of his wits, only replied, 'I see, I see', and went on sewing, 'pulling out' for all he was worth. Seeing this the buggane got angrier still, and his roars grew louder, as he drew his feet up out of the ground and stamped them down on the floor of the church so that the walls shook. But by this time Timothy had put the last stitch in the breeches, and was out through the window and away down the hill. He was only just in time, for the roof came crashing down behind him, and out came the buggane still roaring at the top of his voice, and laughing as loud as a thunderstorm at his own cleverness. The tailor put on an extra spurt of speed, and though it was all uphill, managed to reach the safety of Marown churchyard. The buggane couldn't follow him into this sacred place, and was so furious that he tore his own head off his shoulders, and threw it over the wall at Timothy where it burst into pieces among the gravestones. Timothy lived to tell the tale, but the buggane was never seen again either with or without his head, but as no-one has ever tried to put the roof on St Trinian's again, he may only be hiding somewhere waiting his chance.

The story ends in such a cacophony of fiendish laugher, exploding head and crashing roof, that for most people the notion of seeking some explanation for such extraordinary happenings goes clean out of mind. It occurs to some however to wonder why it was a tailor who set himself to face the buggane, and why it was in St Trinian's that the fiend chose to appear.

Of all the craftsmen mentioned in Manx folklore, it was the tailor, earning his living by travelling round the countryside making clothes, who was the cleverest at getting the better of the fairies, and by far the most likely to hold his own even with a buggane. He had no fear of them and seemed to understand their ways. He recognised a fairy changeling when he saw one, and it was a tailor playing his fiddle who made the seemingly lifeless creature jump out of its cradle onto the floor and dance like a mad thing: when the fairy child stopped dancing to his music and began to 'grin' and cry when its 'mother' came back into the house, the tailor told the woman what kind of a child she had and how to get rid of it and get her own back again. Many other people – weavers, shoemakers, ploughmen, women working in the dairy and in the fields – had dealings with the fairies, and whether they fared well or ill, they were always at their mercy, but the tailor, sharp and bright as his own needles and scissors, seemed to know instinctively how to deal with them.

As for the buggane, it was by its very nature an unknowable creature: only something that has lost its identity qualifies for buggane-hood. An old man who realised that they were sometimes imagined before they were seen, but still a great believer in them, remarked with great perspicacity, 'The buggane, you see, was the thing you were afraid of'. This subjective thinking hasn't deterred some from trying to establish a positive identity for the buggane of Keeill Brisht, even so precisely as to name outstanding figures in Manx history who might qualify. The buggane's appearance as we have it doesn't assist much; 'the mane of coarse black hair,' 'the torch-like eyes', is surely not how people remembered Sir John Stanley, who (some think) might have been responsible for the interruption in the building of St Trinian's, when the Prior of Whithorn to whom the Barony belonged, summoned to come and do fealty for his Manx possessions, and given forty days' grace in which to do it, was one of those who 'came not' and as a consequence forfeited his lands. This was in the fifteenth century and the church's style of architecture requires a buggane of an earlier date. Possibly then at the cessation of Scottish rule when the Island came under English domination. An English king lately at war with Scotland would have been unlikely to confirm a grant of land to a Scottish baron, so when in 1333 Edward III granted the Island to William de Montacute, the Priory of Whithorn may have been dispossessed. The precise date when this happened is not known, though it is on record that in 1604, many years after the Dissolution, the Provost of Whithorn requested unsuccessfully to have the Manx Barony returned to him; though surely not after an interval of two hundred years.

A buggane well capable of bringing the church roof down could have been one of any number of raiders, known and unknown: Richard de Mandeville who, with a body of Irishmen, landed on the Island in 1316 and spent a month plundering the country, then came again a few years later, this time 'with a multitude of Scottish felons', could have been responsible for any number of 'broken' Manx churches.

A pagan origin for the buggane is just as likely as any of

these: an ancient god of some disestablished religion showing his disapproval when a Christian church was built in the place formerly sacred to him. Sabine Baring-Gould, arguing a Slav origin for the North Country Boggarts and bogles (and if he had known of them he would no doubt have included Manx bugganes), derives their names from the Slav word *bog*. 'God is *bog* in the Sclave tongues', he tells us: a god that was brought here by the Danes and Norsemen in the debased form of a demon, a *bug*. He adds that 'the final degradation to which the supreme deity of the Sclaves has had to submit has been to confer a name on a particularly offensive insect that does promenade in the night and proves itself a torment'. The Manx language appears to have insulted this deity further by adding the diminutive *ane* to his name, thus making him into a little god.

The desecration of sacred sites, old churches and burial places, and its consequences was one of the most fruitful themes of Manx folklore, and stories about it could once be heard all over the Island, for the little keeills, the churches of early Christianity, were numerous. Many stood in fields on the farms, enclosed by a *rullick,* or graveyard, but the field known as the 'chapel' or 'churchyard' field was never ploughed, and the keeill itself was left undisturbed. That at least was the people's attitude in theory, but there were despoilers in the past who dared to set the plough among the gravestones, and take the stones of the church to build with. Retribution for such an act was swift and certain, and a man who was guilty of it found himself seized with terrible pain or went suddenly blind or became sick and died. Sometimes whole families were afflicted, and died out. If the stones were used in buildings that housed cattle, the beasts would bellow and roar and take no rest until the stones had been returned to the sacred site. It would probably be no exaggeration to say that of every ruined keeill on or near farmland, some such story was told, though not all are on record. There were even one or two stories like this about St Trinian's: it was said that a stonemason who used a stone from the church in a nearby building and was ill for several months afterwards, recovered when the stone was found and replaced, but a boy who took one away when he was playing round the church died, as the stone he had taken could never be found. It was probably out of a firm belief in the inescapable fate of those who were guilty of misuse of the sacred stones that there arose the old Gaelic ill-wish, *Clagh ny killey ayns corneil dty hie.* (A stone of the church in the corner of thy house), which was the equivalent of a curse.

There were some very remarkable stones of the church, and of the churchyard. The Norse settlers in the Island in the tenth and eleventh centuries were Christianised by the Celtic people they came to live amongst, but the symbols of the new religion were not enough for them: they remembered their own gods, and carved their legends on the memorial stones they erected for the dead.

Stones have been found here depicting Thor going to fish for the world-serpent with an ox-head for bait; Heimdall the warder of the gods blowing the Giallr horn to summon them to their last battle, and Odin with a raven on his shoulder being devoured by the wolf Fenris at the battle of Ragnarök. Yet these stories never became part of Manx folklore; the people seem to have been unaware of their existence, and knew nothing of the legends depicted on the stones, which remained undeciphered until the scholars and antiquarians of the nineteenth century began to look for the meaning of the carved figures and runic inscriptions.

It is strange to think that incidents from the story of Sigurd the Volsung – his killing of the dragon and roasting its heart, the slaying of the otter that was paid for in stolen gold, Sigurd's horse Grani carrying away the treasure on its back – that these and other scenes from a story that was to become world-famous and reach its ultimate development in Wagner's operas, were carved on stones in churchyards in the Isle of Man more than two hundred years before they were first written down by the Icelander Snorri Sturlason in the thirteenth century.

8 The Fairy Cup of Ballafletcher

NOT MANY MILES AWAY in the next parish lived a spirit of more peaceable habits, whose legend has been eclipsed by the activities of the noisy buggane, for its function was unspectacular, to preserve not to destroy, and such an unobtrusive spirit is liable to be overlooked except by those immediately concerned. It had in its care the fortunes of the old house of Ballafletcher in Kirk Braddan. Like many estates in the environs of Douglas and Castletown this house and farm had passed through various hands until it came into the possession of Colonel Wilks, who in his day had also been a guardian of Napoleon on St Helena. Previous owners of the property were a family called Fletcher, and from them the estate received the name by which it is known today. When it was transferred to the new owner, there was also given into his keeping a drinking glass, 'a crystal cyathus, engraved with floral scrolls, having between the designs, on two sides, upright columellae of five pillars'. This glass, the new proprietors were given to understand, was not a Fletcher family heirloom but belonged to the house itself, and must remain there undisturbed in its niche, and descend with the house to successive owners. Colonel Wilks apparently respected the tradition attached to it, for he had it 'encased in a strong oaken box mounted with silver'. The legend was that the cup was associated with a *Lhiannan Shee,* a fairy woman, not in the rôle in which she was more usually found in the Isle of Man, a pursuer and haunter of young men, but as a guardian spirit, a protectress of Ballafletcher, who as long as her cup was preserved in the old house would ensure that all went well with its occupants. But if it was broken she would revert to type and haunt whoever was responsible. It became known as The Fairy Cup of Ballafletcher, and was always carefully guarded, and taken out only once or twice a year when the head of the family drank a health from it to the good spirit of the house.

And that is really the end of the story, for the cup, last heard of in the possession of the Bacons of Seafield, has been lost sight of; the Fletcher family are dispersed, and the old house of Ballafletcher long since gone.

The legend when first published caught the attention of nineteenth-century antiquarians, who found that with a little skilful manipulation of the details, the plot can be made to thicken, and a highly interesting historical background be suggested for the Ballafletcher fairy cup.

The keenest exploiter of its possibilities was H. R. Oswald, a doctor practising in the Island around the middle of last century. 'There is something very interesting in this goblet . . . in connection with the Runic crosses and Runes in the churchyard as well as with the debris of an unknown redoubt and the obscure-looking ruin of a fortified post . . . an ancient encampment which I have lately traced out on the farm of Ballafletcher, Braddan', he wrote in a description of Antiquities of the Parish of Braddan, in particular an 'Ancient Fortalice on Ballafletcher'. In accounts of the Ballafletcher legend, the revelation of the alleged origin of the cup comes as something of a sensation, for when its more recent associations with the various occupiers of the estate have been dealt with at some length, there is usually a brief reference to the supposition that it 'belonged to Magnus the Norwegian King of Man, who took it from the shrine of St Olaf when he violated the saint's sanctuary'.

Having made this rather startling claim for the cup, Dr Oswald goes on to develop an argument in support of his view that the Braddan encampment, is not as might be readily supposed, 'an altar of the Druids' but part of the ruins of a stronghold built by Magnus over seven hundred years ago. The Chronicle of Man and the Sudreys bears this out in so far as it tells that Magnus built three forts in the Island 'from timber brought over by the men of Galloway', but the monks who compiled the Chronicle make no mention of the cup taken from Olaf's shrine, and in fact, according to them Magnus was so terrified, when at his own insistence the tomb was opened and the body of the Saint found uncorrupted by death, that he fled from the scene. As for the forts built by Magnus, it might be assumed that they were built on St Patrick's Isle at Peel since that was where he landed, but no-one knows for certain where they were sited. Such discrepancies apart, Oswald is persuasive up to a point, though his 'highly probables' and his 'seem to indicates' and similar phrases occur too frequently, and when to suit his purpose he changes a perfectly feasible place-name *Chibbyr Niglus,* Nicholas' Well, into a highly unlikely one *Chibbyr Magnus* his case begins to fall down.

He might have done better if he had followed up another line of thought, which had evidently occurred to him since he mentions it in passing, but surprisingly makes no further reference to it – the former history of the farm of Ballafletcher itself, which must be taken into account by anyone assuming a Norse origin for the cup of the Lihiannan Shee. The farm was part of the Barony of the Bishop of Man and the Isles, and its name before the Fletcher family gave it theirs was Kirkby, a name of Norse derivation meaning the farm or estate of the church. The tenants of the Bishop's farms were required to pay dues or 'customs', certain quantities of grain, livestock and turf, which they did as always when this was required of them by Lord or Baron, with great reluctance and a bad grace. Still more resented than this regular payment was an obligation on each estate to supply 'a choice ox' whenever a new bishop was consecrated, and when as happened between

1633 and 1663, there were four new bishops within the thirty years, this 'benevolence' (as it was called) became an exacting imposition. It was said at the time that a bishop who was sick could always feel well assured of his tenants' heart-felt prayers for his recovery.

There was one farm belonging to the Bishop's Barony that was exempt from these obligations, and this was Kirkby, whose tenant instead of paying customs was held responsible for the entertainment of the Bishop on his visits to the Island: 'He pays no custom, for this only, to entertain ye Bopp. at his Landinge or Going away'. This traditional service seems to have been well-known and remembered among the people, and folk etymology, seldom found wanting when a neat explanation is required, claimed that the name Kirkby or Kirby as it became later, arose from the farm's long-established duty of providing food and lodging for the Bishop, and actually derived from the Gaelic *Cur Bee*, meaning 'Give food'.

The origin of the Fairy Cup must necessarily remain unproven, but, significantly, its legend is associated with Ballafletcher, the old estate of Kirkby on the Bishop's Barony, and the connection suggests a possible means whereby it could have come to the Island. Dr Oswald implies that Magnus himself brought it, but he is so intent on proving how the Norse King could have sailed his boats inland to build his stronghold in Braddan, that he forgets the fairy cup and fails to follow up the link between it and the archaeological remains which he suggested in the first place. His theory was however taken up and developed by Sophia Morrison in her fairy story *King Magnus Barefoot*, in which she tells how the King went away from the opened shrine of Olaf but 'took with him the lovely crystal cup that lay beside the Saint', then came to the Island where he built his three forts. 'In one of them, near Douglas, he placed the Cup of Peace, which he knew would be well guarded by the Lhiannan Shee the peace fairy who never left it.'

There is one rather weighty argument against the possibility of Magnus having had anything to do with the opening of the shrine: in the Saga the story is told not of Magnus himself, but of his grandfather King Harold, that 'on the eve of his sailing for England in 1066, he had the Shrine of Saint Olaf opened, cut the nails and the hair of the Saint, and having re-closed and locked the shrine, threw the key into the sea; it is expressly added that the shrine was not opened for the next one hundred and eighty years, so it is impossible that Magnus could have done it [which the Chronicle of Man says he did in 1098]'. The writer of this note undermines the historical basis of the Fairy Cup's origin, though he concedes that the story of Magnus' opening of the shrine 'may have been a legend or tradition current in the Isle of Man'.

Assuming that the cup existed, and this has to be accepted as Dr Oswald not only describes but illustrates it, there is another possible or at least permissible theory of its connection with the house of Ballafletcher. It seems reasonable to suppose that it could have been brought by a Bishop travelling from the Isles to Man, and placed for safe keeping in the house at Kirkby on the Bishop's own lands. Whatever holy influence may once have been believed to surround it and its preservers, could then with the passage of time have changed to a supernatural but benevolent oversight by a mysterious Lhiannan Shee.

It may or may not have been a cup used by Olaf or Magnus: drinking vessels of ceremonial use seem to have existed in Viking times and later. Scott had heard of the like and in his *Lord of the Isles* anyone who gets as far as the Second Canto can read the Lord Ronald's demand:

> 'Fill me the mighty cup,' he said
> 'First owned by royal Somerled'

– though the massive 'Hebridean drinking cup of ancient workmanship, long preserved in the castle of Dunvegan on the Isle of Skye' of Scott's note seems to have been a very different kind of vessel from the Cup of the Lhiannan Shee which Oswald described as 'uncommonly light and chaste', and which he thought 'might pass for a specimen of the glass of ancient Sidon'.

The King Magnus connection with a drinking cup is curiously persistent. Further on in his notes to the Lord of the Isles, Scott refers to an inscription on the Hebridean cup which mentions 'Magnus Prince of Man' but the date 993 is a hundred or more years out, though one commentator, determined that it shall be relevant, thinks it could justifiably be read as 1093.

The Fairy Cup may have had no such miraculous origin: it

may perhaps have been brought home by some seafaring Manxman, an early example of the many mementoes of their travels that Manx sailors were to bring back from foreign lands. But however it came, its story belongs to the old estate of Kirkby as surely as the buggane's does to St Trinian's.

These legends of the Baronies are true examples of the 'gossamer' of folklore that Roeder spoke of. The events out of which they grew are long since lost sight of; the stories, left to drift and wander have miraculously survived, and from time to time someone has attempted to bring them down to earth and set them on a solid though never very certain foundation.

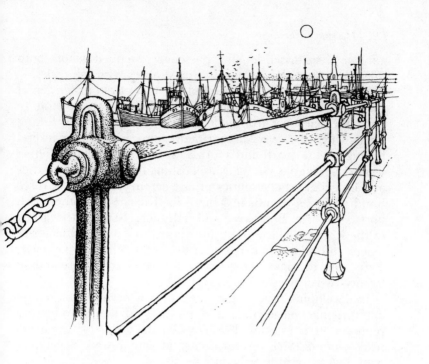

9 Herring Fishermen

FISHING BOATS STILL go out on late summer evenings from the harbour at Peel, past the castle on St Patrick's island and round the breakwater, then head south for their summer fishing grounds off the south-west coast. As the season advances the herring shoals shift northward up the east coast from grounds off the Calf of Man where they gather early in the year, and even in a bad season some of the best fishing can be found in late summer and early autumn on this side of the Island. Of late years record catches were taken at this 'back fishing', as it is called, the boats crowding into the harbour in such numbers that they had to wait their turn to land their catch at the quay. The harbour at Douglas was so congested that there was no room for the passenger boat from Liverpool to berth, and when she was due the fishing boats had to retreat into the bay, so that the steamer, grown suddenly to the size of an ocean liner, could edge her way in through the small craft thronging the harbour entrance. From the gangways surprised-looking passengers stepped ashore onto quays strewn with herring nets and slippery with fish scales.

Scenes like this bring to mind the talk of old fishermen of the days when at Peel and Port St Mary it was possible to cross the harbours from side to side on the decks of fishing boats, when they were preparing to go to the spring mackerel fishing off the south and south-west coasts of Ireland. These were the great days of the Manx fishing fleet in sail, the sixties and especially the seventies of last century, when over three hundred boats set out in March for Kinsale and other Irish ports, Valencia, Berehaven and Baltimore. Some of the fastest of the Manx Nickies, built and rigged in yards and factories chiefly in Peel, a smaller proportion in the other fishing ports, were able to make the journey to the south of Ireland in twenty-two or twenty-four hours.

In developing this fishing, the Manx fishermen, backed by enterprising boat-owners and builders in the Island, were pioneers. It is estimated that, when the industry was at its peak around 1880, several thousand people were dependent on it directly or indirectly for a living.

Mackerel fishing on this scale was a nineteenth-century innovation, but to the herring fishing Manxmen were born and bred. The hymn sung by the Peel men before the fleet put to sea:

> Our wives and children we commend to Thee,
> For them we plough the land and plough the deep,
> For them by day the golden corn we reap,
> By night, the silver harvest of the sea.

has become part of Manx folklore, and is invariably sung at Harvest Thanksgiving services, but it is nevertheless a mere nineteenth century afterthought and the piety of its sentiments,

> Like them of old, in vain we toil all night,
> Unless with us Thou go, who art the light,

is only a half-truth. No-one would attempt to deny that there was a very religious element among the Manx fishermen, some of whom were devout Methodists. There were certain religious rituals that were never omitted: one that might have had Methodist inspiration was called by the crews 'finishing the day', when every man on board when the nets were shot at night, got down on his knees and prayed, or had a prayer said for him if there was 'a praying man' among the crew. But long before the days of John Wesley, the herring fleet had never gone to sea without the church's blessing, for it had a very real interest in the herring fishing and its outcome. The ceremony of blessing the fleet was presided over by the Bishop himself, and there was a special form of service for this quayside benediction of the fishing boats before the herring fishing season opened, which in earlier days was not until the middle of July. The fishermen themselves were ready to go to the herrings when they had finished their spring sowing and planting,

When the barley's sown, and the potatoes down,
Then we go at once to our boats.

Their wives and families did the rest of the work on the crofts, for some of the men went on fishing well into the winter.

When the Peel fishermen were clear of the bay and within sight of the Calf of Man, they used to raise their hats as a mark of thanksgiving – but to which god no-one seems very certain. For once he was at sea a Manxman began to show his allegiance to deities unknown to those on land, and they were of many kinds. One of them was probably the sun, for when they turned their boats at the harbour mouth. It had to be sunwise: a fisherman preparing to paint his boat was observed to be stirring the paint pot only towards the right. Reverence was paid also to 'coul' iron', for iron was the remedy when anyone on board infringed the prescribed code of conduct by saying or doing things that were forbidden, and there were many of these. There was also the *Dooinney Marrey*, the Merman, and the terrible monster known as *Yn Beisht Kione Dhoo*, the Beast of Black Head, that was dreaded by all who sailed the southern coast. Everything in the boat acquired magical properties as a repository of 'luck', not only important objects like the fishing gear, and the cran baskets and the tally-stick with which the catch was counted, but even the dish-cloth, and if any of these were lost or stolen or lent the luck of the boat went with them. The Manx fisherman believed in having the best of both worlds, pagan as well as

Christian, practising a religious eclecticism that left nothing to chance, and this mixed creed he inherited from generations of his predecessors over many centuries.

The Manx herring fishing is long established, its laws dating back to the thirteenth century, and so deeply entrenched is the herring in Manx life and traditional consciousness that it was regarded and used as a symbol of the impartial administration of justice. In old Manx law the oath taken by the Deemster or judge, when he is appointed to office, requires him 'to execute the laws of the Isle justly ... betwixt party and party as indifferently as the herring backbone doth lie in the midst of the fish'.

The reason for the herring's importance was that for centuries it was the people's main food, eaten with various kinds of bread made from oats and barley, and later with potatoes. The finding of the herring shoals each year was literally a matter of life and death, and as the time of year approached when the herring would be expected off the island, the people watched the signs eagerly and anxiously, and in the early days horns were blown when they were sighted.

On sea we would be watching for signs of herring, such as gannets, perkins and such-like. But gulls were our best friends, that is why there is law that they must not be shot. The signs of the gulls were always minded. The best sign is to see them lying in flocks upon the water, making a noise, and turning their heads about; then rising, flying and settling down again. The young gulls are far keener for fish than old ones. We would be watching the signs of the gulls on land too, on Monday morning when coming down from the country to our boats. For the gulls would be going higher or lower on the hills as the fish shifted out off (land). But when they went up the river we knew it was time to go round for Douglas back (fishing). Some of the men were putting these signs down, making an almanac of them, for the week. But the best of all the signs is to see the 'li'l silver fellas' themselves. On a dark night if you came over a body of herrings, the water would be all lit up with them, and you would see them shining and glittering underneath the waves.

Even the behaviour of insects was significant: a daddy-long-legs flying about early in the year was 'a sign of fresh herring', and when the *lhemeen y skeddan,* the herring moth, was seen flying round the house in the evening there would be good fishing that night. This continual reading of signs and the constant watch kept on wind and weather are more understandable when it is realised that the whole Island once depended for survival on a good herring season. Sometimes and for no obvious reason the harvest of the sea was so bountiful as to be almost an embarrassment. In 1793 'the herring were so abundant that they were caught with the hand on the beach, after being sold at 4d a hundred; purchasers could not be found, and they were carted off for manure.' But just as unaccountably it could fail, as it did repeatedly in the seventeenth and eighteenth centuries, and these failures coupled with bad harvests sometimes brought the people to a state of near starvation and famine. In the Book of Common Prayer in the Manx language, there is included a petition which was first introduced by Bishop Wilson after a period of great scarcity of herring in the early years of the eighteenth century, that it would please God to 'restore and continue to us the blessings of the sea', a form of prayer that came to be regarded as the normal Manx version of the Litany.

When the fishing failed in Manx waters the fishermen did not rely solely on prayer to remedy their fortunes. It was as a direct result of these times of failure that they went further afield in search of new fishing grounds. It was said of the Manx fishermen that they would go wherever there were fish, and this enterprising spirit led to wider experience of seafaring and enabled them to develop the skill as seamen and fishermen for which in the nineteenth century they became noted.

Little is known about the Manx fishermen and how the fishing was conducted until the seventeenth century when in 1610 a law was enacted 'for the better regulation of the herring fishing', which the act pronounced to be 'as great a blessing as the Island receives', providing the tenant farmers with 'the wherewithal to supply their wants and occasions when as all their other Endeavours and Husbandry would scarce advance any such Advantage and Gains unto them'. The act had many subsidiary clauses regulating the conduct of the fishing and of

the fishermen, and the seemingly urgent need for the
introduction of reforming measures and the nature of them
suggest that the Manx fisherman of this period was an unruly
character and the fishing grounds something of a battlefield.
By implication they are accused of fouling each other's nets,
cutting off buoys and corks, stealing or 'shaking' herrings out
of other men's nets, striking each other and 'drawing Blood by
violent Strokes' and of uncharitable language. There is even a
suggestion that the herring fishing had lapsed altogether, as in
the same year it was found necessary to question 'fower
ancyent men, Mallo Calloe, Willm Kerush, John Christian
and Willm Corran, who perfectlie did remember the Herring
Fishing in the Isle'. They were not apparently fishing on the
Manx coast, but described themselves as 'fishers driving for
Hearring in the North of England with Mancks Boates'.

These old men recalled the obligation on every quarterland
to have 'always in readiness prepared for the Hearring
Ffishing eight fathoms of Netts furnished with Corks and
Buoys . . . conteyning Three Deepings of Nyne Score Meshes
upon the Rope'. The word 'Deeping' for a section of net of
certain dimensions has remained in current use, Manxified as
'jeebin' and people still speak of 'making jeebin'.

Just how nautically minded Manx people were before the
Norsemen came and developed and encouraged whatever
sea-going propensities they may have possessed is hard to say.
Not much is known of early Manx vessels: the bog-oak canoes
that have been found here were probably used only on rivers
and inland lakes and marshes. Charles Roeder is convinced
that the Manx, like other Celtic peoples, once had a wicker
boat of the 'currach' type, and states boldly: 'The Manx word
for the wicker boat has long gone out of date, but a dim
allusion is contained in the Manx word *currag* or *corrag* which
means a bundle of osiers'. Osiers certainly grew and were
grown here and were extensively used by fishermen and
farmers for basket-making and many other purposes, and it is
not inconceivable that they may once have been grown and
used for boat-making. Osiers are commonly called 'sallies',
but on those quarterland farms where they were grown, the
small enclosure allotted to them is always on record as 'the
osier garden', never 'the sally garden'.

The earliest type of boat known in the Island was
undeniably of Viking ancestry. It was called a *scowte,* a word

deriving directly from the old Norse word *skuta*. It was large enough to accommodate nets and other gear for fishing, was pointed at both stem and stern and carried a square sail. It was this sail that gave it its later name, when in the eighteenth century it became known as a Squaresail to distinguish it from the boats of fore and aft rig that were coming into use, both for fishing and for trading. The old laws mention 'herring scowtes' and 'small boats' as two distinct types of craft. While the former were used exclusively for herring fishing, the 'small boat' was in all probability a smaller version of it and used for the line-fishing for cod and other fish from the small creeks and beaches about the coast. Many Manx people today speak of 'a small boat', by which they mean a small rowing boat.

This chapter begins with the rather misleading picture of the herring boats setting out for their night's fishing – for these are in fact no longer Manx boats, but mostly Scottish, and English, and it is they who now supply the herring both for local consumption and for the considerable kippering industry that is carried on in the summer months. The Manx herring fleet for reasons both economic and political has dwindled lamentably over the years and its surviving remnant has gone over entirely to the more profitable, nine months of the year escallop fishing. It may seem strange that the Island's herring fishermen should have been content to relinquish an industry with centuries' old traditions behind it, inherited and handed down from father to son, and surrender their fishing rights in Manx waters to the 'stranger'. The stranger was in fact no stranger, for he was always with us participating in the fishing and in other Island affairs. As a fisherman in Island waters, he, like the Manxman, had to pay his proportion of the custom herring, the Castle Maze. The Manx fisherman had to pay one *mease* (that is a long hundred or 124 herring) out of every five, and 'the stranger' was proportionately assessed. The stranger fisherman attracted to the shores of the Island in a good season probably helped to widen the Manxman's horizons and gave him new ideas – as the Norsemen had done; for on any new fashions in the rig or design of boats he was quick to seize, and modify and improve them for his own purposes, no matter where he found them or came by them. It was by this process of working on new ideas that the fishing boat known as the Nickey evolved which came into use for the mackerel fishing in the nineteenth century, and was said to have been modelled on and named after the boats of Cornish fishermen.

The Island's early boatbuilders observed many of the old sea taboos and superstitions:

> In old times we used to build our boats in the country anywhere near trees; timber where the fairies were talking was lucky to build with ... A silver piece, or a bit of iron would be put under the stern post for luck sometimes. When the boat was ready to be caulked we would have to turn her over with the sun, a boat must always go with the sun, going to sea, especially, if you can come at it in the world, go out with the sun!

In those days boats were built in many a creek round the coast, some even in the glens. Some boatbuilders in Perwick used to leave off work in the cave they were using as a boatyard, so that the fairies could come in to work. Whether the fairies on the night-shift there made any useful contribution is not on record.

Potatoes and herring continued to be eaten by many people in the Island until at least the pre-war days of this century. Each summer in July or August, when the fish were at their best, 'the stock' was salted down for the winter in crock or barrel. Some farms would have a whole *mease*, 620 herring put down to feed both family and farmworkers. They were eaten several times a week, and some farmworkers got very little else, a cause very often of bitter grievance and rather rueful humour: after an unrelieved winter diet of herring the menservants on one farm claimed that they could shake herring bones out of their shirts.

There is no doubt that the salt herring has lost its former lofty symbolic status in the Isle of Man. It is now the symbol of poverty especially in the official mind, and the worst fate with which a Manx politician can threaten his constituents is 'a return to a spuds and herring economy' – the inescapable alternative to whatever scheme he happens to be cherishing for the Island's immediate salvation. The situation is, however, rather ambiguous as far as the people are concerned, for nurtured on salt herring as many undoubtedly were, they are now supposed to have outgrown their taste for them, scorn them as an article of diet and since they can afford it, live on better fare. To keep us from returning to 'spuds and herrin'' large sums of public money have been poured into many schemes, few of them good, the rest either bad or downright disastrous, and each in turn envisaged as the final panacea for the Island's economic ills. The Island itself is in process of being carved up by builders and developers – this too so that we may become rich and prosperous and be preserved from having to eat 'spuds and herrin' ever again. The opinion of the mass of the Manx people, which is on the whole disregarded, is that soon they will have no land left to grow the potatoes, for it too is passing into the hands of the 'stranger' and of a different type from the one who has taken over the fishing of the 'herrin'. The truth of the matter is that the ordinary people of the Island would probably welcome a return of at least some of the simplicities of the spuds and herring days, and anyway they haven't stopped eating them; they may not salt them down any more, but the fishmongers sell them by the dozen all through the winter.

One of the returns made by the Clergy for the considerable benefits they received from the fish tithe that they insisted on having, was to hold a service to bless the fleet before its departure to the fishing grounds. This the people expected and indeed it was obligatory by Canon law. Bishop Wilson, Bishop of the Manx Diocese from 1698 to 1755 compiled 'A Form of Prayer to be Used at Such Times as The Fishermen in the Diocese of Mann can be Gathered together for Divine Service during the Herring Fishing', in which God is asked to preserve them 'from the dangers to which by their calling they are exposed . . .' as Noah and his family in the Ark were saved from Perishing by Water'. The Bishop, finding himself among a seafaring people and living almost on the edge of a stormy coast, was probably more fearful for the fishermen than they were for themselves; so conscious was he of the dangers of the sea that he had a special private prayer in readiness to recite on behalf of those at sea when a storm blew up: 'O God who of thy good Providence has appointed me my portion in this Island where every storm puts me in mind of ye dangers they are exposed to who follow their business upon ye seas . . .' There must have been many occasions for its repetition.

The Rev. J. L. Stowell, Vicar of German in 1841, with the town of Peel in his parish, and with less exalted expectations of the fishermen and more understanding of their real nature, had his own methods of dealing with their backslidings. He called them together and exhorted them in 'An Address to the Fishermen of Peel on the Reasons for Gratitude and Thanksgiving to God for their Safe Return from a Prosperous Fishing'. First of all he recalled the tragedies of the past – six men of the fleet lost in 1833, ten in 1821, eighteen in 1781, and in 1787 'twenty-one souls lost at the herring fishing in Douglas Bay'. He reminded them that by the mercy of God they had not suffered a similar fate but were 'still spared to stand on praying ground'. Then, having made clear their obligation to heaven, he demanded: 'If you have been duly grateful for your safe return to your families and firesides, what means the drunkenness, what means the profane swearing ... what means the Sabbath-breaking?' Bishop Wilson was careful to include prayers in his fishermen's service that would prepare them for unsuccessful seasons and preserve them from self-congratulation when times were good, so he warned them that God 'may suspend his blessings for a time, to make us value his favours . . . and to convince us that we depend upon his providence entirely, that we may not praise ourselves, and like the Philistines worship our own nets'.

Whether this constant surveillance by the Church over the fishermen's moral state was necessary or not, the clergy never let up, they never released the moral pressure. The Rev. Stowell terrorized them into repentance, threatening them in one of his sermons with a terrible picture of the fate of 'mariners who all unprepared are engulphed in a watery grave'. 'Shall I attempt to give you a moment's insight into the abyss of perdition,' he asked, 'and show you in the deep a lower deep?' The admonishings of the Church, even such heartless exploitation as this of the very real dangers they had to contend with, had their effect on the fishermen, and they earned a reputation for piety. 'A loving and simple-hearted people' was John Wesley's opinion of them when he preached once to a gathering of Peel fishermen.

But for all their religious observance, piety and prayer, they never relinquished old customs that were totally at variance with the religious teachings of the Church of England, and when they were at sea, or going to sea, their attitude to the Clergy was unequivocal: they wanted nothing to do with them. To meet a Protestant clergyman when a man was setting out on a Monday morning to his boat was only slightly

less unfavourable than to meet a woman. To meet either was
very unlucky and the fisherman who had the misfortune to
encounter one or the other of them felt he might as well go
home, as he was convinced he would have no luck all day.

Whatever the more obscure reasons for the parson's
unpopularity at sea and it may have been because he was a
priest of a religion inimical to that of the old sea-gods to whom
the fisherman instinctively began to do homage as soon as he
set foot in his boat, there was a more obvious reason in the
amount of the catch that in former days had to be handed over
to the Church as tithe. From early times the Church had
insisted on this and on their own exemption from payment:

> the Bishops shall have their Herring Scowte and their
> Fishing Boate, freely and frankly without any Tythes
> paying wheresoever they land in this Isle. In like manner
> . . . the Abbot, the Priors the Archdeacon. Alsoe all Parsons
> . . . shall always choose their Fishing Boate at Easter and
> their Scowte at Herring Fishing time, whether their Fishing
> be about this Land or Elsewhere . . . Every Master of every
> Fishing Boate shall cause all fish to be brought above full
> Sea Mark, and there pay truly the Tythe. Also when
> Herring Fishing is, the Proctor shall take his Tythe where
> the Boat doth ground or land.

No matter what the state of the fishing, in good times and bad,
the State and the Church between them exacted from the
hard-pressed fishermen about a third of their catch: '40-45 per
cent', one writer estimates, 'went like a flash in the frying pan
before they could touch a single fish.' It is small wonder that
the fish tithe was always a cause of resentment and rebellion
among the fishermen. Even the rocks round the coast had
unfortunate associations with the Clergy. Rocks that went by
names like *Creg yn Taggyrt*, Parson's Rock, *Creggyn Jaghee*,
Tithe Rocks, were avoided by men fishing about the coast, as
tithe had to be paid out of any fish they caught there.

Another cause of resentment among the fishermen was the
state of the harbours and landing-places round the coast. In
spite of their profits from the fishing industry, neither church
nor state exerted themselves to improve the fishermen's
conditions by providing better harbour facilities. The landing
places round the coast were many of them very dangerous,

and the town harbours were neglected. A direct result of this was the wrecking of the herring fleet on 21 September 1787. The previous year, the pier with its light had been swept away in a gale, and only a lantern slung on a pole was there to guide shipping to safety. On this September night as the fleet were coming in, a sudden squall arose, and one of the boats knocked down the light; the rest lost their bearings and were swamped by the rising sea.

Some time after this tragedy in which 23 men lost their lives, a local poet wrote about it in lines of truly McGonagallesque quality, saying with some justification,

> Had the Pier at Douglas been re-built,
> This misfortune had not been,
> And it really is most scandalous
> That the ruins still are seen.
> Ships and boats pay certain dues
> The harbour to keep in repair;
> Pray then why not repair our harbour
> And re-build our quay and pier?

In fact nothing was done about the harbours until the fishermen themselves took action in 1880, when on Midsummer Fair day 1500 of them marched in procession behind a brass band to Tynwald Hill, and stated their demands. The fishermen never forgot the wreck of the fleet in Douglas bay, and on the night of its anniversary, 21 September, they didn't go to the fishing.

It is perhaps just as well that the parson was strictly taboo both in person and in name aboard the herring boats, as the greater part of the fisherman's customary practices were wholly pagan. How many of them would have been presented at the Chapter Court and sentenced to penance, fine and imprisonment, and accused of all the sins in the book, if the parson had witnessed such ceremonies as the burning of a witch out of the boat, or the pouring of a libation to the Beisht Kione Dhoo? The ritual for driving a witch from a boat was as follows:

In the evening when the nets were in the water, if it was calm, they got a lot of oakum and tied it on the end of a stick, then soaked it well with tar in the tar-bucket. When the darkness set in they lighted the oakum and the tar, and the skipper took the torch and commenced at the stem-head and the rest of the crew looked out for the witch. The skipper went with the torch to every place where they said the witch was and put the burning torch in that place. They kept going from one place to another for a long time, until someone said the witch was gone aft. Then the skipper went aft with the torch, and put it in every crevice round the stern sheets until the witch was on the rudder-head, he said, and then she had to get off that too from the torch, and jump in the sea. Then the skipper threw the torch into the sea after her.

If a boat was having bad luck at the fishing the skipper would send to Nan Wade or Teare Ballawhane for herbs.

I would be sent to old Charles Teare Ballawhane for herbs. We would have to boil them in a pot, and every one of the crew would have to drink a drink of it – mighty bitter stuff it was too; then the rest of the liquor with the herbs in it would be thrown over the nets. Sometimes the luck (the herbs) would be tied to the tail of the net.

They made a special meal of the first herring that was caught:

The first herring on board the first night out at sea would be boiled whole. The other herrings in the pot would have their heads and tails cut off. We called the first herring *yn eirey* [the heir, or first son]. When it was cooked every man on board would have to come and take a pick of *yn eirey*.

Of all the creatures that haunted the sea-caves, the one most dreaded by the fishermen was the *Beisht Kione Dhoo*, the Beast of Black Head. Some of them believed that it was the spirit of a man who had been murdered by some pirates so that it would guard the treasure they had hidden in a cave on the headland, and they used to hear it roaring in its cave when they were out pulling ling on Spanish Head. One or two had caught sight of it and said that it had a head like a big horse. Some of them, when they were sailing down the coast towards the Calf of Man, would stop and leave some rum in the cave on Spanish Head where the *Beisht* was, as a kind of offering, and that brought them good luck at the fishing: and when there was a tot of rum going on board, they never forgot to pour some over the side for the *Beisht Kione Dhoo*.

There was a very precise code of conduct to be observed when at sea. Many a young boy making his first voyage as cook on board a boat going to Kinsale or up to the Shetlands, had to be reprimanded for whistling at his work. Whistling, it was believed, 'bothered the wind' and even in calm weather the wind was never whistled up. The approved magic for raising it was to stick a knife in the mast on the side from which it was desired that the wind should blow. In days long past there were witches in the Island who sold wind to seamen bound up in the knots of a length of thread. The sailors were permitted to loosen two of them, but if the third knot was undone it would unleash a hurricane and they would be shipwrecked.

It was particularly unlucky to lose things belonging to the boat, or to give them away. Fishermen were always trying to get the luck from others' boats, asking if they could borrow matches or salt, and they would even take a handful of thatch from the house of a successful skipper, to transfer his luck to themselves. Some would give nothing away, they wouldn't even tell the time to a man in another boat.

Many of the 'haaf-names', or sea-names, that were used are forgotten now, but no four-footed creature was mentioned at sea: rabbit, hare, cat and rat were never refered to by their usual land-names. They all had to be spoken of by strange circumlocutions like *fer lesh cleaysh liauyr,* fellow with the long ear, a hare, *scraaverrey,* scraper, a cat, and *fer yn famman liauyr,* long-tailed fellow, a rat. This last is often heard today, for many people, whose former connection with the sea lapsed long ago, still call a rat 'a long-tail', and there seems to be a general ingrained reluctance to speak of it by its land name. An old fisherman recalled how when he first went to sea this strange lingo was quite unknown to him:

I went on the boats a greenhorn from the plough. It was natural to me to talk about animals, but I found that it wouldn't do. To talk about a horse or a pig was awful, an' a hare or a rabbit. One night I said something about a horse, an' the sailor on deck with me laid hold of me by the ear and rushed me down the companion to the engine room. 'Coul' iron', he was sayin', 'Coul' iron! You mus' grip it tonight!' I had to take a nut of the boiler between me teeth before I could get rid of the evil that was in me mouth.

Fairies and Roman Catholic priests were exempt from these prohibitions. If the fairy fleet were seen on the water there would always be a shoal of herring where they had been, though the boats themselves would disappear at daybreak. There was no ill-luck in meeting a Roman Catholic priest as the fishermen believed he had 'some sort of power over things of darkness, spirits and the like.'

Mermaids and mermen were on the whole well-disposed towards the people on the land. The fishermen particularly were well acquainted with them and their ways, and knew how to keep on the right side of them by giving them a dishful of herrings or any other gift they fancied. The mer-people had fore-knowledge of the weather, and the crew of a boat who were on good terms with them would be warned of storms to come. There was once a herring boat that was manned by a crew of seven single young men; she was called *Baatey ny Guillyn*, The Boys' Boat. Every place that they shot their nets they got herring. Her crew though young were canny, never forgot when they were hauling their nets in the morning to throw a *jystful*, a dish of herring overboard, so they were well in favour with the people of the sea and always had good luck. The Admiral of the fleet saw that they were doing better than the other boats, and he knew this was causing jealousy and trouble among the crews, so he made them come to Port Erin shore and take oath that they would truthfully tell the rest of the fleet where they were getting such good catches. The Boys' Boat crew swore that they always fished south of the Calf, so the whole fleet made for that ground. When they had their nets shot, the young men on the *Baatey ny Guillyn* heard a voice saying quite plain *'Te kiune as aalin nish, agh bee sterryn cheet dy-gherrid'* ('It's fine and calm now, but there's a storm coming soon'). So they put their nets on board and made for the harbour. No sooner had they got in than a sudden squall arose and swamped the rest of the fleet; only two escaped and they almost drowned trying to save their father. It was given for law after that that no crew should consist only of single men: there had to be at least one married man on board. And no man was bound in his hiring to fish in the Southern sea, which was known as the Bloody Sea ever after.

At the end of the herring fishing season, the *Shibbyr Baatey* was held, the Boat Supper, traditionally on St Stephen's Day or New Year's Day of the old Calendar, and the wives and sweethearts of the fisherman were all invited. It was known also as *Yn Scoltey,* The Parting, presumably the parting of shipmates until the next fishing season. It is not all that well remembered now, but there was one memorable Boat Supper, when after the feast the fishermen acted a play to amuse the company, about a night at the herrings. They 'shot their nets' by spreading them out on the ground, then put their oars through a hedge and made believe they were at sea, and went through the whole performance of a night's fishing; looking for signs of fish, shooting the nets, and finally losing a man overboard. The spoken dialogue was all in Manx, and even in translation is full of obscure fishermen's terms, the peculiar language of the haaf-fishing.

'Were you proving there boy?'
'They refuse to mesh!'
'How much are you pulling out of the pair?'
'About a hundred'
'It's just as well to prove again.'

In the middle of the performance a storm gets up and they decide to pull in the nets: 'It's as well to put on board, it's looking wild.' Then the climax of the play: 'There's a man overboard, A boat! A boat!'

'Throw a rope to him!'
'He's going down a second time!'
'I have him! I have him! Hold him sure, lift him on board!'
'Catch hold of him by the hair of the head,'
'Grip him by the neck!'
'Is the breath in him?'
'He is coming to!'
'Put him across on the barrel, and let the water run out!'
'He was near death!'
'A man will not be drowned if he is to be hanged!'

10 Three Places

THE SEA THAT HAD ALWAYS provided a means of livelihood
for the Island gave opportunity for other pursuits, some of
them far less innocuous than fishing, while the wilder more
inhospitable places further inland provided what can best be
described as fringe benefits which people were very ready to
take advantage of. The old people had a saying that there were
three places where you could make a living, in the currraghs,
on the hills, and by the sea. This was wisdom gained from the
hard experience of life of less prosperous islanders, not so
much the view of the solid well-to-do farmers and substantial
landowners – though they too were well aware of just what
riches lay concealed in such places for those who knew how to
obtain them, and they were not above availing themselves of
them from time to time.

In the first two, the curraghs and the hills, they could find
many of the necessary materials for living, for building their
houses particularly, and because many people had little or no

transport, they built them in these out-of-the-way places so that they would be within walking distance of their sources of supply. Their greatest need, apart from a roof over their heads, was fuel for cooking and heating: light they could do without, and often had to, but fire they had to have. Though many used sticks gathered from the hedges for their fires, especially gorse 'bons' (for the gorse had many uses apart from gladdening the eyes when it was in bloom), the fuel generally used throughout the Island was turf, as it is always called here. There were two kinds that people could get, one that was dug out of the curraghs, often in very wet situations, and the mountain turf, which was preferred, as it could be cut under drier and pleasanter conditions, and was of better quality. The annual excursion to the turf ground was one of the great social working occasions, and even when turf was no longer burned, and the need for it was gone, the labours and pleasures of the days spent cutting turf on the hills were often called to mind, and in time became proverbial, so that when anyone engaged in strenuous work, beyond their usual routine they would say they were having 'a big turf-mountain day'.

Whole families set out for the turf ground on the first of May to cut the year's supply of fuel. Each district had its own particular ground, and the roads leading to them can still be followed though they are no longer used except by walkers. They are back roads from the farms branching upwards into the hills, converging onto the main tracks crossing the mountains which lead to the turf grounds on the Rheast, on Clagh Oury, Barrule, Beinn y Phot and several others. There was always keen competition for a good site, and a start had to be made at daybreak or before to get there in time. The usual means of travel was in horse-drawn carts, and whole convoys of a dozen or more would be seen setting off for the mountain in the early morning, and returning again at night, though some camped on the mountainside. Some idea of what it all looked like can be gathered from an account written at the end of last century, which though fictional is well-observed:

> To be first on the ground meant the choice of the best cuttings, and long before dawn the whole country was up and away to be on the spot by sunrise. It was a jollification of hard work and of feasting – a bivouac on the brown mountain waste of hundreds of country carts and

thousands of folk, fires blazing, kettles steaming, frying-pans hissing, round-bottomed pots bubbling, universal hailings, greetings, laughter, courtings – for women, girls, and children are all there by prerogative right . . . The folk from the distant northern plain camp all night on the mountainside, each family with a cartload of bedding, and a sailcloth rigged over the carts. These night campers are the envy of all. The song is sung and the tale told with pipes and stone jars of ale around the fires; and the old men are to the fore recounting the doings that went on in the past days.

The turf-cutters of much earlier days did not use the field-kitchen equipment described on this occasion. The food traditionally eaten on the mountain was a dish of *cowree,* a kind of porridge that was quite simply prepared. Oat husks and a sprinkling of oatmeal were steeped all night in water, which next day was strained off and boiled until it thickened, and when cold boiled up again with milk; it was this not very substantial-seeming dish with which hard-working turf-cutters once fortified themselves at midday. It was also a favourite food of the fairies who seemed to approve its combination of simple ingredients, and liked to find a dish of it left ready for them when they made their nightly visits. Once, when fairies went to a house to look for supper, they found nothing prepared for them; the *cowree* dish was empty, and they were so disappointed that they spat in it, hoping no doubt that this rather unmistakable sign of their disapproval would serve as a reminder, a sufficiently unpleasant one, for future occasions.

By the latter part of the nineteenth century people were no longer reduced to an oatmeal and water diet at the end of the winter. Their dinner on the turf-cutting day was more likely to have been a fine potful of Manx broth warmed up over a fire. The children who went to the mountain may have helped with the work, but for them it was very much of a picnic excursion, a day out on the hills they had hitherto only seen from a distance. The adult members of a party working on Clagh Ouyr missed the children during the midday break, and discovered that they had taken advantage of their already high situation to climb the remaining thousand or so feet of nearby Snaefell, and then, worn out with the climb on top of their morning's work, had lain down and fallen asleep on the summit.

Turf-cutting was hard work with neither shade from the sun nor shelter from the wind, and by evening everyone was ready to stop and lay down their tools – the *faayl,* the long-handled feathered turf-spade and the slatted hand-barrow like a small funeral bier on which the cut turf was carried to the drying ground – and straighten their backs and go home, leaving the result of their day's work strewn around the turf-lag in the first stages of its weathering and drying.

The turf from the curragh was very wet to handle and it had to be handled a good deal, 'baked' by women wearing sheepskins for protection. The use of cooking terms in the processing of curragh turf is misleading as no heat was applied; the women shaped the wet turf with their hands into *bonnags,* or round cakes, then laid these out on the meadowland to dry in sun and wind as was done with the turf from the mountain, where some days after cutting, the small blocks were set up on end, three or four together so that the wind would blow through and around and dry them out. The turf was carted home for stacking usually after harvest, so that for almost four months of the year it lay out on the mountain, a temptation to the unscrupulous. Turf-cutting had always been controlled by strict laws, from whose content it is obvious that a good deal of pilfering and stealing went on at times under cover of the mountain mists. In 1661 it was

> ordered and declared that no Manner of Person or Persons shall presume to go to the Mountains or Commons of this Isle after the Hour of Five of the Clock in the Afternoon, or before Day in the Morning for the carrying away of any turf or Ling, for that Complaint has been made, that some Persons do frequent that Course, and espetially upon Dayes of Haddy or dark Mist, and do purloyne and carry away Neighbour's Turf and Ling at such unseasonable Times; wherein if any do offend for the future they shall be severely fined and punished as by the Court shall be thought fitt.

Not everyone was able to go to the mountains for firing, so they went instead into the fields and along the roadside hedges to gather *bons,* or sticks, chiefly of gorse which they carried home in a *bart,* a bundle on their back. A Manx emigrant on a

visit to the Island after long absence in America was disgusted
to find that the children in the village where he was born
didn't know the meaning of the expression 'a bart of bons'. In
the years he had been away 'going on the bons' had been one
of his most cherished childhood memories, and it seemed to
him that to have forgotten or worse still, never to have known
the vocabulary of such a highly traditional pastime
symbolised a loss of nationhood. Many of the people who
emigrated in the early years of this century took with them
and retained a mental picture of life in the Island as it was
when they went away, kept it fresh in their minds, regarding it
lovingly from time to time, happy to think of life going on the
same as ever in 'the li'l island'. Then after thirty or forty years
they came back and found that things had moved on in their
absence, and the Island of their dreams and memories had
vanished. Their disappointment, even indignation, would
have been pathetic if it hadn't been laughable, when they
discovered that while they had been away among the
skyscrapers, the little shop where they used to buy their
pennyworth of Manx peppermint 'knobs' had gone out of
business, and old Ann Jane living up the road, who had given
them fresh-baked oatcake and soda-cake when they ran up the
path to her front door, was long ago in her grave, and there
was almost no-one left who lived in the way they remembered
– in a thatched house with flagged floor, and dresser against
the wall, and pot-oven and griddle over the fire on the hearth.
This homecomer with his memories of 'going on the bons'
would have appreciated as a scene from only yesterday the old
Manxwoman in a poem by Cushag, sitting by her fire of gorse,
and brooding over her past life and her present loneliness:

> It'll be in the 'teens of years I'm livin' here alone,
> An' the home is bare at me now like a nes' when the
> birds is flown;
> But the days is lonelier far pas' what it is in the night,
> For then I'm stirrin' the bons till the house is full of
> light.

And this was often the only light they had then, or the dim
glow of the 'slut light', which was a rag-wick in a scallop-shell
full of oil, and the glimmer of a rushlight in its iron holder.
Even the glow of the tallow candle or the fairly considerable

light of the paraffin lamp would seem inadequate today,
though in the Isle of Man some of these early means of lighting
have not all that long been put away, and have occasionally to
be brought out again when electricity fails in storm or stress of
some kind. There is perhaps less of a tendency now to think of
objects like these as primitive and entirely outmoded bygones
to be consigned to the never to be returned to past. They
sufficed in their day and could do so again.

If people in the Island today, even the most resourceful,
were to be set down in the places and circumstances in which
their ancestors lived, they would soon acquire a new
understanding and respect for their skill and knowledge and
adaptability, and as rapidly come to realise how ill-equipped
they themselves were by comparison to cope with such
conditions. Between their day and this a whole science of
living has vanished. In their chosen territories – the curraghs,
the hills, and the seashore – they were almost self-sufficient,
finding the materials needed for living ready to hand, and
turning them all to good account. A use and purpose could be
found for all things that grew or could be dug out of the
ground: sedges and rushes or bent-grass for thatching, osiers
for basket-making, wood and stone and clay for building, long
strips of grassy turf with which they lined their house roofs
under the thatch, bracken and fern for bedding their cattle or
to burn for ash to bleach their linen, and many other things
necessary to their way of living.

Though most people did not possess the more esoteric
knowledge of the fairy and herb doctors, they knew the
simpler medicinal uses of many plants and the magical
properties of some of them. Around old houses and farmsteads
plants can still be found growing in deserted gardens and
among the cobbles of the farm 'street', seeded from herbs that
were once grown for medicinal use in a variety of infusions,
salves and poultices. Yarrow is one that is often found, with its
white or pink flowers and feathery green leaves, a herb that
was commonly used to heal wounds, and taken for colds and
coughs and asthmatic complaints. To the yarrow an unusual
measure of respect was shown, especially by young women
and girls, who when they found it growing gave it a polite
greeting, 'Good morrow green yarrow, good-morrow to thee',
and if they gathered it by moonlight and slept with it under
their pillow, they would dream of the man they would marry.

Comfrey was also regarded as a herb of healing, and was used in the treatment of bruises and sprains. Clumps of it can be found flourishing in old gardens where it was planted long ago, with blue and purple flowers, and leaves rough on one side and smooth on the other, which if placed on a wound in the right order would first draw and clean and then heal it. The herb vervain was the most magically potent of all, an antidote to every kind of evil influence. Everyone knew of its power and virtue and carried pieces of it in their pocket or hidden among their clothes, and no-one was properly equipped for a journey or any other enterprise without a sprig of vervain.

There were several plants used in food preparation, *Lus ny Binjey*, Dropwort, *Lus y Steep*, Spearwort, gathered in marshy places and both necessary ingredients in the preparation of rennet for cheese-making and for binjean, the plain Manx junket eaten in summer when milk was plentiful. The plant Sundew, *Lus y Druight*, was alleged to be an aphrodisiac, as its other name *Lus ny Graih*, Herb of Love implies. It was obviously thought of as a herb of great power to compel and attract, as it was known in Manx by yet another name, *Lus yn Eiyrtys*, Herb of the Following, or as some translate it, Herb of 'the certain consequences', but unfortunately there are no known instances of its power in operation, except in fiction. To many people now *Lus ny Graih* is not a plant, but a dialect play, once very popular, in which one of the characters tries out the magic herb and finds that it works.

Samphire that grew profusely on some of the most dangerous cliffs was a fringe benefit and one that people risked their lives to obtain There is a story told of two samphire gatherers, a husband and wife, who were one day working on the cliffs at Spanish Head. They caught sight of a particularly fine bed of the plant growing on a ledge of rock below them, but well out of reach. Unable to forego such a prize the man got a rope and tied it round his wife and lowered her down the cliff. That she made the descent might seem significant, but probably only meant that she could not have held her husband on the rope. The woman reached the ledge safely and gathered as much samphire as she could put in the bag she had taken down with her, then signalled to her husband to haul her up again. As he did so, the inevitable happened; the rope, perhaps an old one, worn and frayed with friction against the sharp rocks gave way just as she had nearly reached the top and she fell to her death on the rocks below. They were probably gathering the samphire not for their own use, but for sale, as people gathered so many things to sell at the fair or the market to make a little extra money.

It is probable that the dizzy heights and fearful overhangs of the rocks held less terrors for those who used them than they do for people today. Fishermen walked daily on paths to the shore which seem scarcely negotiable now, and wildfowlers poked puffins from their holes on the cliffs and climbed for gulls' eggs in situations of great height and hazard. The miners and quarrymen thought little of working on the very brink of the cliffs: the way down into some undersea mine workings where men were employed in the last century were right on the cliff edge, and at a quarry on Spanish Head lintels were cut from the rock face hundreds of feet above the sea, and lowered with ropes into a boat waiting below. Men who had to work in places like this had strong nerves, and of necessity kept them and their imagination, as far as physical danger was concerned, under strict control.

There is one tradition of the rocks and headlands around the Island that it might be preferable to leave untold. It is almost too horrible to mention, and all the more so as it is no legend but based on historical fact. It belongs to the north-east coast and especially to the Kirk Maughold cliffs where there is a place called *Slogh ny Gabbyl Screbbagh*, The Pit of the Scabbed Horses, and it was here old people say that sick horses were taken and backed over the cliff. It is strange that the tradition should have attached itself only to this spot as the old law giving the instruction specified no particular place: 'If there be any manner of Person or Persons that keep any scabbed Horse or Mayre . . . the Coroner ought to bring them to the next Hough and cast them down' – according to which any precipitous part of the cliff would have served the purpose. But, though it may have been done in other places, the name is found only on the Maughold coast.

When this barbarous deed was last done and when it ceased is not known, but it was done, and old people speak of it with revulsion, not as a personal memory, but as something they have heard, impressed on their minds by its horror and the picture it conjures up of the diseased and terrified animal driven to its death step by step backwards over the cliff. It might have been said some years ago that such merciless cruelty is no longer conceivable, but twentieth-century methods of torture and slaughter enable the assertion to be made with less confidence. Such a desperate remedy for contagious disease could never be justified, and it can only be hoped that the individual was more merciful than the law required him to be.

Wrecks were frequent in the day of sailing ships, especially in the storms of winter and with onshore winds, and the people of the Island understanding the sea, and knowing well the dangers of the coast were always ready to help ships in difficulty and to save lives while risking their own.

Such rescue attempts are part of the people's history, a duty they never shirked, and it is necessary to stress this fundamentally courageous and humane attitude to shipwreck, since to wreck in the more restricted legal sense they took a more business-like attitude; they were always on the look-out for whatever the sea might bring to their doors, the *mooircheeraghyn*, the flotsam, especially from wooden ships, whose timbers in an island once almost treeless were a valued and much coveted prize. Some of them can be seen yet, long heavy baulks of wood in use as gateposts and lintels, deeply pocked with round holes that formerly held the trenails, or treenails, the shipbuilders' word for the wooden pegs that fastened them together. In the roofs of many older houses, especially farmhouses, the purlins and joists are of ships' timbers salvaged from wrecks of a hundred and more years ago, which occasionally betray their origin by taking on in damp weather a faintly silver sheen of salt.

Wreck had always been the prerogative of the Lord of Man, as it became later of the Crown, but this did not deter the people from flocking to the shore when a ship was wrecked or grounded for whatever spoils were to be had. The harvest through the years was rich and varied, cotton bales, sacks of flour, boxes of fruits, tea, sugar, barrels of oil, assorted crockery, casks of spirits, coal and bricks . . . Rhymesters of varying talent were fairly common in the Island at one time, who exercised their gift in writing mainly for their own and others' amusement about local events and affairs, and in wrecks they found considerable inspiration as an exciting topic in itself, and also enabling them to expose and satirize the greed and covetousness of their acquaintances. To quote from their verses might even now be libellous, as personal identity was often only thinly disguised; but a village poet, who made no secret of his jubilation at the riches provided when a boat carrying a miscellaneous cargo was driven onshore on the east coast, probably spoke for many when, having enumerated the various commodities left strewn around on the beach, he concluded,

> O that another might be found
> With general cargo, outward bound!

The coast of the Island has a folklore of its own; it was haunted by unidentifiable spirits, an 'infernall Spirit' that 'would so affright passengers with hydeous noyses and cause such disturbance in ye waters in ye night time, yt many ships were thereby wreckt', and the *cughtagh* which though not anonymous, was little more than a voice, and yet believed to be 'an evil spirit whose abode was in the caves by the sea, and whose voice was the coughing and whispering of the waves'. There were stories also of submerged islands: one was situated off the north-west coast at Jurby, but most of them lay off the south-east, and the traditions about them are strongest around the Langness peninsula. Sailors and fishermen reported that, when they were far out in the bay and well beyond reach of any noises from the land, they would hear bells tolling and the sound of human voices and the bleating of sheep coming up from the depths of the sea where it was supposed an island lay buried. Once in seven years it rose to the surface and it was said that, if it stayed long enough for someone to place a Bible on it and so sanctify it, the enchantment that held it submerged would be broken and it would never disappear again. This had been tried but without success as no-one had got there in time. One night a young man and a girl were walking by the seashore when the girl whose name was Onny Maddrell suddenly caught sight of the island lying on top of the water some distance out in the bay. Without a word she left the young man standing, ran home and snatched up the Bible and hurried down to the shore with it, but as she got there and before she even had time to get into a boat to row out to it, she saw the island beginning to sink down into the sea, and in no time it had gone. The saddest thing about this mysterious island was that if a person tried to reach it with the Bible and break the spell but failed to get there in time, the enchantment turned against them and in a little while they became sick and died. Onny Maddrell did not escape the fate of others before her who had tried and failed, and within a year she was dead.

These legends of lands beneath the sea puzzled the more rational-minded, and attempts were made to give this particular island and the vicinity where it was supposed to lie a name and historical background. The historian Camden was probably responsible for the misconception about the 'Fane of Sodor' which he equated with St Michael's Isle near Langness, where he said 'Pope Gregory IV instituted an Episcopal See, the Bishop whereof, named Sodorensis (of this very Island it is thought) had jurisdiction in times over all the Islands'. This apparently authoritative statement laid the foundation for subsequent theories, of which the most circumstantial was advanced by a local historian at a time when most antiquarians were still baffled as to the significance of the word Sodor in the Bishop's title and in the name of the Diocese of Sodor and Man.

> The south of the Island was the Diocese of Sodor and the town of Sodor was on Langness . . . the Bishop of Sodor lived in that town and the fishermen had to bring their tithe to him. After a time however, the plague came to the town and the people had to set fire to it and leave it. I have heard from some old people that there was a great storm fifty or sixty years ago, which laid bare several of the foundations of the houses of Sodor and that they were flagged or paved with red freestone, but that the sand and grass covered them again.

Such stories were no doubt founded, however confusedly, on some already existing tradition, and must in their turn have added substance to the rumours of mysterious islands and vanished cities which seem to belong to the Langness peninsula particularly and to the south east coast in general. There is probably no stretch of sea-coast that does not have its traditions of a lost Lyonesse, and of sunken cities from which the tolling of bells and the sounds of the human world are heard, but there cannot be very many of them that have such eminently distinguished ecclesiastical connections. This report of the former now submerged 'See of Sodor' was taken note of by a nineteenth-century Manx Bishop who apparently thought it was time to settle the matter of 'Sodor and Man' once and for all, which he did in facetious but not too pontifical verse:

> What does the title Sodor mean,
> Pray tell me if you can,
> So strange are many facts we glean
> About the Isle of Man.
>
> That all the cats are wanting tails
> We hear for ever-more,
> It may be this accounts for tales
> That reach the British shore.
>
> Well, 'Sodorenses', Southern Isles,
> Is what the title means,
> Although perhaps you say with smiles,
> Tell that to the marines!
>
> For in the palmy days of old,
> When things went harum-scarum,
> The Bishop did the title hold,
> Of Man – et Insularum.

The whole of the Island's rocky coastline lends itself to fantasy and gives scope to the imagination, and it is to be wondered how much the appearance of the rocks themselves has contributed to the stories of spirit-haunted caves and headlands on lonely rock-strewn beaches where the sea breaks in on monstrous forms, and the out-going tide leaves them sprawling, seaweed-covered and sinister at the foot of the cliff. These ancient rock masses have a presence of their own, and at Langness are sea- and weather-worn into shapes strange and fantastic enough to make even a geologist close his professional eye for a moment and see instead of the schists, conglomerates and porphyritic granites of his normal vision:

> uncouth faces outvying the poppy-heads of mediaeval architecture ... grinning down upon you from every nook and cranny. Gigantic noses, gaping mouths fashioned out

of the boulders and white quartz pebbles which protrude from the red mass of the conglomerate, topped with rude wigs and hoary lichen moss and saxifrage. There is one isolated mass which has oft reminded me of the dons of our ancient English universities on commemoration days in cap, wig and romantic robes . . .

Yet, in spite of these urbane and academic resemblances, their closest similarity is to a jagged row of teeth bared skyward right round the peninsula, that on stormy days with an onshore wind were death to the ships driven in on them. Memories and ghosts of the drowned still linger round this corner of the Island, and Langness itself, with past associations not only of storm and wreck but of ancient battles and pirate raids, is even yet an unquiet coast. In days gone by the bodies of the drowned were never buried far away from the tide-line, as people were reluctant to take them from the sea that had made its claim on them, and some lie in the graveyard that surrounds the little twelfth-century church on St Michael's Isle at the far end of Langness. Here the ghost of a sailor used to be seen sometimes coming up at dusk from the water's edge, a kind of representative wraith of all who had drowned there. A man living in Castletown said he had 'seen him times, a sailor in ribbons and shoes coming up from the shore about sunset, and seen him go up the land'. Further round the coast, another used to be seen when darkness fell, sitting brooding on top of his grave above the rocks.

The light from the eastern window of St Michael's church, built on the island within a pebble's throw of the sea, must often have served as a guiding beacon to sailors along this shore, but not all who saw it came with good intent. The church is roofless but its walls still stand, threatened now only by the salt-laden winds that sweep over them from every side. In past centuries it was exposed to continual danger from the sea, and tradition tells of a raid on it long ago by pirates who murdered the priest and seized his treasure, and then were drowned themselves getting back to their ship. The church is said to be haunted; the sounds of the pirate raid and its slaughter never left its walls but stayed imprisoned in the stones, and anyone who knocked on the outside wall would hear them again, cries and groans and curses, and the jingling of coins.

There were times when the people's urge to go to the cliffs and the seashore for what they could find was thwarted. Certain parts of the coast were the preserve of the Lord of Man who had not only his game Forest on the hills, but his Warrens round the coast and the people's access to and use of such places was restricted by law. 'We give for Law that Whosoever goeth to the Forest either by Day or Night to kill my Lord his Game, he ought to pay vjjl for every one of them.' and on the coast 'the houghs', as the cliffs were called (an old name still used sometimes for the headlands by the sea), were at certain seasons of the year specially guarded from intrusion by the populace, as it was there that the falcons so much prized by the Lords of Man had their breeding ground. 'We give for Law that whosoever goeth to the Hough where the Hawkes do breed, or Hyrons likewise, he forfeiteth for every one of them, if he take any of the old or young Ones or Eggs, iijl a-piece.' When the Island was granted to the Stanleys in 1406 it was on condition that they present two falcons at the coronation of each King of England 'in lieu of all other Services, Customes and Demands'. This service the Lords of Man, both Stanley and Athol continued to render until the reign of George IV, at whose coronation it was reported that: 'Amongst the feudal services, the two falcons from the Isle of Man were conspicuous. Seated on the wrist of his Grace, the beautiful peregrine falcons appeared with their usual ornaments. The birds sat perfectly tame ... completely hooded and furnished with bells.'

Because of this ancient service, there has been a tendency to claim for the peregrine falcon the romantic-sounding name in Manx, *Shirragh yn Ree,* Hawk of the King, and with such a long-established custom as the presentation of the falcons, there seems every reason why it should have acquired the name, but it is highly doubtful whether the people ever used it, and the vernacular name for the peregrine seems to have been merely 'shawk'.

11 Smugglers' and Other Tales

MOST OF THE FRINGE BENEFITS enjoyed by the people were sanctioned by law and custom; they were an integral and legitimate part of their culture. But there was one, by far the most lucrative, that was of more sudden development and sanctioned by no authority. This was the smuggling for which the Isle of Man became notorious in the late seventeenth and eighteenth centuries. It was in fact hardly a fringe activity, for during the hundred or so years that it was carried on the whole Island was to some extent involved in it and dependent on it – merchant, landowner and fisherman.

It is not surprising that the Island, strategically situated in the middle of the Irish sea, should have become a smuggling centre. Its suitability for the purpose was recognised by a group of adventurers who came over from Liverpool with the express intention of exploiting its potential as a safe and convenient centre for the landing of cargoes for re-shipment to places on the surrounding coasts. The Island was a separate kingdom with its own laws and tariffs; the King's writ did not run there and ships once within a certain distance of the shore were beyond the reach of revenue officials. George Waldron soon found how powerless he was to intercept boats once they were 'within the piles'.

> I myself had once notice of a stately pirate that was steering her course into this harbour, and would have boarded her before she got within the piles, but for want of being able to get sufficient help could not execute my design. Her cargo was indigo, mastic, raisins of the sun and other very rich goods which I had the mortification to see sold to the traders of Douglas without the least duty paid to his Majesty.

The legal position in the early years of the eighteenth century was stated unequivocally by counsel at the time: 'I am of opinion that no Officer of the Customs can by Virtue of any Deputation from the Commissioners of Customs in Great Britain make a seizure in the Isle of Man, because as I take it, their Commission does not extend to that Island.' The low import rate into the Island compared with the much higher rate on the mainland made smuggling worth while, and doubly so, as there were other shipping monopolies and restrictions on imports in force at the time that if they did not justify smuggling at least provided excuse for it. It is officially unadmitted, but fairly generally accepted, that the improvement in the rig of sailing vessels, particularly the introduction of the fore and aft rig, were brought about by the need for greater speed and mobility when running cargoes into and especially out of port, as with the old squaresail vessels crews were unable to make a quick get away after landing goods but had to wait for a favourable wind; the fore and aft rig enabled them to take advantage of any wind and sail immediately. It was a change that would have come about anyway as it was of benefit to the fishing industry, but the requirements of the vessels engaged in the 'running trade' hastened it on.

There are stories told of how the smugglers succeeded in

outwitting the revenue men. A cargo that was brought ashore on the west coast was hidden in a field of cabbages where an old man was working, and when the revenue officers, hot on the smugglers' trail arrived there, the only reply he would make to their enquiries as to the whereabouts of the hidden cargo was *'Fo nyn gassyn'* ('Under your feet'), so, either failing to understand his Manx or thinking him half-witted or possibly both, they went away. This cargo had been landed by a boat called the *Moddey Dhoo*, whose master was the notorious Quilliam of Peel. It was said that he used to lure the customs men into pursuit just for the excitement of the chase and the pleasure of leaving them behind. The *Moddey Dhoo* was nearly as notorious for its speed as he was for his daring, and once when he drew the Revenue sloop after him and raced it half round the Island then got away with ease when he had had enough, it was said that he had previously greased the bottom of his boat with bad butter. More stories are told about Quilliam than about any other smuggler. His races with the Revenue men were probably not without purpose; his speed enabled him to act as a decoy and draw them away and keep them in pursuit as long as he pleased, until it suited him to be 'caught' when all they would find on board would be a *mollag*, or float, full of sea-water, while meantime his confederates had been able to dispose of the real cargo, mollags full of spirits. Acting the innocent or the simpleton, like the man in the cabbage field, was a favourite device with smugglers for fooling the customs officials. Quilliam once took up his stance at the foot of the Nelson monument in Liverpool, and gathered a large crowd round him and kept their amused attention while he offered sea-biscuits to some bronze negroes on the monument – while his men were delivering some smuggled brandy safely to its destination. The story of the skipper who fends off the searchers by saying that he has cholera on board is also told of Quilliam.

The bladder and the mollag, or skin float, were the Manx smugglers' great standby for transporting spirits. It is scarcely to be wondered at that few tales were openly told of how the cargoes were landed and transported to their destination. It was a secret business and carried on as unobtrusively and with as little publicity as possible,. often by night. Something of the smugglers' methods can be deduced from the measures that were taken against them. In an act of 1825, a good number of years after the sale of the Island to the British Crown, every possible aspect of the trade was reviewed and brought under control, and all that had previously been secret and hidden was revealed and defined, and forfeited.

> Vessels discovered in bays, creeks, harbours or rivers of the Isle of Man or within one league thereof, having on board Goods liable to forfeiture, to be forfeited together with such Goods and Packages . . . Vessels sailing from the Isle of Man with a greater number of men than is allowed, or taking on board small cordage more than is usual or necessary, or tincases, bladders etc, adapted for smuggling to be forfeited. Boats belonging to Vessels to have the name of the Vessel painted upon the outside of the stem, and the Master's name on the transom.

Goods were to be shipped on days 'not being Sundays or Holidays, and in the Daytime'. 'If any Tea, Spirits of any kind whatsoever or Tobacco shall be brought to or found on any wharf or other place with intent to be waterborne for Exportation, the same shall be forfeited together with the Horses and other Cattle, Carts or other Carriages employed in removing the same.'

These were precautions aimed at the whole procedure of smuggling, and though they seem merely the bald facts of the law's requirements, the hitherto untold tale of the smugglers' activities can be deduced from them – the small unidentified boats running quietly by night into creeks and coves; the horse-drawn vehicles ready waiting to take the cargo overland to its hiding or storage place; and the cargoes frequently broached and stowed into small containers that could be easily handled, distributed and concealed. There were larger measures directed against boats converging on the Island from all quarters without 'cocket' or customs' clearance, and other requisite marks of legality, and a clause dealt also with the transportation of cargoes within the Island, which the law equated with re-export.

These journeys must have taken place secretly and in darkness, and there are no accounts of the routes taken nor any description of incidents on the way, and it would seem as if no-one who was involved in the traffic ever told of it. It may be that the 'death coach' that the old people talked about, the mysterious cortège that made its muffled progress over country roads at dead of night, may have covered some of the activities of smugglers. The ghostly vehicle was heard but rarely seen; it was as if nobody dared to investigate it, or else deliberately refrained from doing so. It is possibly in this form that the people remembered 'the Horses and other Cattle, the Carts and other Carriages' that the law so clearly identified. The phantom coach was heard on several roads in the Island, usually travelling only one way. There is a tradition of it in Malew parish on a winding upland road, in which some mishap is involved, a vehicle overturning at an awkward corner on the narrow road. In Port St Mary a coach and horses were heard driving down towards the harbour, but were never heard returning. If it had anything to do with smuggling and people knew what was going on, they never admitted it. Here as elsewhere 'the gentlemen' went by deliberately unregarded. Considering how near to us in time, comparatively speaking, the smuggling days were, this gap in knowledge particularly of their doings on land, for there are a fair number of sea stories of smugglers, is remarkable It is as if the whole Island at the time was united in a conspiracy of silence, in which there were no informers.

Smuggling no matter where it was carried on, inevitably became shrouded in romance, and was made to appear the great adventure it probably never was. In this the Island was no exception, and while the true facts may never be known, a background of picturesque scenes and incidents has by some inexplicable spontaneous means been created as its setting.

Among the most popular of these fantasies were the smugglers' caves associated particularly with the east coast. At the southern end of the shore at Laxey a 'cave' now blocked by a fall of earth could once be explored, candle in hand, for a fair distance, and it was rumoured that it used to be possible to follow it underground for a mile or so, and that it 'came up under the churchyard'. It was only a step of the imagination then to hear a boat being run up onto the little beach below (the iron ring where it could have been tied up is there in the rock, though worn and rusty now) and see the smugglers climbing the slope to the mouth of the cave with their cargo, making for their hiding place in the churchyard. There might be a slight mingling of traditions in such a tale. Not far away at Maughold some time last century a tomb in the churchyard was used as a hiding place for part of the cargo from a wrecked ship. Given a combination of such likely ingredients as a tomb filled with stolen goods, and a secret passage in the cliff, a smuggler's tale was bound to result. Did children invent these stories and tell them to each other? They probably did, and still do: small boys scrambling among the rocks and coming upon the little creek below the cave were overheard to remark one to another that they supposed this was 'a smugglers' cove'. By this time, and after reading many adventure stories, coves and caves must all have been used by smugglers. In the Isle of Man, the coves may be more genuine haunts of smugglers than the caves, as many of these are nineteenth century mining trials and borings.

Yet this coast must have been used by smugglers, and creeks and small harbours in other parts of the Island. It has been said that the nearest approach in the records to a 'smugglers' cave' is a mention of a landing at 'Ballaugh burn-foot'. The more romantic smuggling associations may be very largely fictional. In *Guy Mannering,* Scott denies any factual basis for his smuggling scenes: 'many corresponding circumstances are detected by readers of which the author did not suspect the existence.' yet he admits that Dirk Hatterick's apparent prototype, apparent that is to his readers, not to him, 'is considered to have been a Dutch skipper called Yawkins. This man was well known on the coast of Galloway and Dunfriesshire . . . his vessel was frequently freighted, and his own services employed by French, Dutch, Manx and Scottish smuggling companies.'

Manx smugglers were sufficiently well known on the coast of Kirkcudbright for a stretch of water there to be known as 'the Manxmen's lake'. The Dutch skipper Yawkins must have been equally well acquainted with the coast of the Island, and it says much for Scott's influence that what originally was probably a folk memory of Yawkins himself, should on both sides of the channel have become associated with his fictional rather than his real self. There is a 'Dirk Hatterick's cave' on the coast of Galloway, and one also in the Isle of Man in the Glen above the little east coast beach at Garwick where it used to be one of the Glen's chief tourist attractions. There were local men who could recall being required to equip this cave with an old grate, a few iron bars and rum puncheons and other oddments for the convenience and accommodation of Captain Dirk Hatterick of the *Yungfrauw Hagenslaapen,* rather curiously described by Scott as 'half Manks, half Dutchman and half devil!', who announced himself as 'all in the way of fair trade – Just loaded yonder at Douglas, in the Isle of Man – neat cogniac – real hyson and souchong – Mechlin lace, if you want any – Right cogniac – We bumped ashore a hundred kegs last night.' On the shore below there is another cave that has a reputed association with a 'real smuggler', so perhaps Yawkins himself is remembered there, after all.

In some quarters it is held that several of the supposed Manx fairy stories are in reality smugglers' tales. There is the story about *Ooig ny Seyir,* a cave on the west coast, that got its name Coopers' Cave because the sound of hammering used to be heard from it, and people said it was the fairies making barrels for their herring fishing, or – fairy carpenters building boats, and some said it was coffins that were being made by the fairies, and they were not for themselves. The sceptics won't accept any of this, alleging that the cave was probably used for a very different purpose by smugglers, and its fairy reputation deliberately encouraged to keep the inquisitive away. Though there may be some justification for thinking along these lines, it takes for granted a good deal of naive credulity on the part of customs officials; and, as it is also suggested that some of the stories Waldron heard were largely fabricated for his benefit, to cover up the illegal activities of his informants, assumes also a high degree of inventiveness on the part of the smugglers themselves.

It seems unlikely that caves would be used as actual hiding places for the goods landed, they were far too obvious a choice, and as easily accessible to the searchers as to the smugglers, and hiding places further inland seem far more feasible, cellars for instance. The characteristic Manx house was usually built on top of the ground, without having a foundation dug for it, and supported on huge boulders for foundation stones. A cellar was not at all in the Manx tradition of house-building, yet some eighteenth-century farmhouses had them, the cellar and the flight of stairs down to it below the level of the flagstone floor. Houses and buildings in the towns of Douglas and Peel which were the real centres of the running trade, particularly the older parts around the quays and harbours, were equipped, it is often said, with a whole network of underground tunnels, passages and vaults, for the landing, concealment and storage of goods brought in. It was a kind of smugglers' architecture that developed over a lengthy period, built and financed by prosperous merchants for the furtherance of their shady purposes.

The smugglers undoubtedly did work underground, but it is taking the rationalist approach to superstition too far to affect to see behind the stories of the wonderful and even the fiendish inhabitants of the underground passages and chambers in the castles of Rushen and Peel only the inventive minds of wily smugglers working deliberately for their own ends on people's natural credulity and fear of creatures of another world. It is far too simple an explanation for the castle stories, but supposing that in some instances it can be accepted, and they were the authors of some of them, they showed themselves to be inspired masters of deception. It was a stroke of genius to introduce the *Moddey Dhoo,* the terrible black dog into the guardroom and dark passages of Peel Castle. Some have said that Scott was the first to do this, but though both Shakespeare and Scott were responsible for peopling the castle at Peel with real and imaginary inhabitants who have lived on in its traditions, the Moddey Dhoo is not one of them. It was Waldron who first reported him in the castle, and it is the only place where this haunter, usually of lonely roads and in almost every sighting, of the outside world, appears indoors. No-one would question its hauntings elsewhere, as it was a dreaded and all too familiar apparition, 'as big as a calf and with eyes like pewter plates', making sudden appearances to travellers on country roads late at night.

The Peel Castle *Moddey Dhoo* stirred the imagination of all who heard of it, and the story of its appearances there has been told and re-told, yet this 'spectre-hound' of the western coast doesn't seem from Waldron's account of it to have been noticeably spectral in appearance, only 'a large black spaniel with curled shaggy hair', quite a dog of this world. It became so regular in its visits to the soldiers in the castle guardroom, coming in each evening and sitting down before the fire, that they grew almost accustomed to it, though they never went near it, and none of them would stay with it or risk meeting it alone. Each night when the gates were locked two of them always went together to deliver the keys to the Captain of the Guard, as the way led through a passage in one of the old churches within the castle walls where the dog used to be seen coming out of its lair. One night a soldier who had been drinking and was reckless and full of false courage began to taunt the others for their fear and credulity, and although it wasn't his turn, said he would take the keys to the Captain himself, boasting that he wasn't afraid of the dog, but hoped it would follow him as he intended to find out whether it was dog or devil. The others tried to dissuade him from going alone, but he ignored their advice, refused all offers of company, snatched up the keys and went out of the guardroom. Whether he delivered them to the Captain or was beset on the way the story doesn't say, only that 'in some time after his departure a great noise was heard, but nobody had the boldness to see what had occasioned it, till the adventurer returning, they demanded the knowledge of him; but as loud and noisy as he had been in leaving them, he was now become silent and sober enough, for he was never heard to speak more.' In three days he was dead, and though while he lived his friends tried to get by word or sign what had happened to him, 'nothing intelligible could be got from him, only that by the distortion of his limbs and features, it might be guessed that he died in agonies more than is common in natural death'.

Through Scott's elaboration of the story in Peveril of the Peak, the fame of the Black Dog of Peel Castle has no doubt gone half round the world, but in the Isle of Man the *Moddey Dhoo* has kept to its old habits, haunting its usual places on the roads, unaffected by the publicity given to this not very characteristic member of its species. Its story has not died out even yet, for people still seem to see them, or did until a few years ago. A man claimed to have met one on a road where the *Moddey Dhoo* was known to be 'taking' when he was going one night to post his football coupon, and he was not surprised when he had no luck.

The *Moddey Dhoo* of Peel Castle was never seen again, but no-one would attempt to go through the passage in the church that it frequented and where the soldier met his end, 'for which reason it was clos'd up, and another way made'. This all happened Waldron says 'about 1666'. There is little or no evidence to suggest that the Castle at Peel was ever used by smugglers, but if the passage that was blocked up was ever one of their thoroughfares, they might possibly have decided that it or others they frequented needed just such a Cerberus to guard it from intruders.

These stories of the castles in the Island always seem to be set in their deepest parts or even further down in the earth itself, as if they belong to an earlier phase of their history and to a structure that long ago disappeared beneath the present buildings. In Castle Rushen these lower regions 'had never been opened in the memory of man', but 'the natives of the Isle used to relate how the castle was inhabited first by fairies, then by a race of giants, until Merlin expelled some of them and bound the rest in spells which will be indissoluble till the end of the world', and presumably the sleeping giant, 'the prodigious fabrick' that Waldron's traveller found during his exploration of the castle's depths, was one of this spellbound race.

It was not only in castles that sleeping giants were found. At the foot of South Barrule there was a Giant's Cave, and 'in the days of enchantment persons were confined there by Magicians, and there is still in that place a great Prince who never knew death but has been bound by enchantment for the last six hundred years, but in what manner he lies and in what form, none ever had the courage to explore'. This place was known as the 'devil's den', and no-one would go near it, and an animal, horse or dog brought to the mouth of it would sweat and start with terror. Strange noises were heard there, and once a dragon, 'with eyes like two globes of fire' and so huge that its approach 'darkened all the element', was seen to disappear into it, and soon after groans and shrieks issued from its depths.

Dragons do not normally belong to Manx tradition, and though a dragon of this description might have been considered an effective deterrent by smugglers using the cave, with the shrieks and groans as added discouragement, there was no need to provide an enchanted Prince; indeed the possibility of finding such a being might have made the curious even more curious. When it comes to stories like this, of some kind of Manx Barbarossa bound in an enchanted sleep, the smugglers must be relegated to their proper concerns and some different explanation be sought for.

Comparisons to these Manx stories of spell-bound giants that come to mind are the legends of King Arthur sleeping in Avalon, and of Merlin bound by enchantment in the forest of

Brocieliande. One folklorist however, Lewis Spence, considers the story as it is found in the Isle of Man to be even more basic, and adds to these the maimed king of the Grail Legend, and attempts to prove that all three derive from a much older common source, the key to which he finds in the story of the sleeping giant of Castle Rushen.

He quotes Plutarch's mention of a traveller Demetrius, who when visiting the uninhabited islands around Britain is told of one where Cronus is imprisoned with Briareus guarding him while he sleeps, 'for sleep is the bond forged for Cronus'. Spence explains the discrepancy of finding a Greek god mentioned by name in British tradition by supposing that 'the name Cronus given by Demetrius to this sleeping deity can only have been his translation of a British appellative'. In Greek myth Cronus was banished to a British Island in the farthest west. Spence's suggestion is that it was to the Isle of Man, in the depths of Castle Rushen.

If this were true, what a triumph for Waldron's 'prodigious fabrick' – to be accounted the sole source of some of the most famous and enigmatic legends in Celtic Literature and Mediaeval Romance. But it is too large a claim to make; the Manx story is an example of, and may be compared with, all such stories of sleeping kings, giants, gods and magicians, but there are scarcely grounds for assuming it to be the prime source of them all.

About that other coastal pursuit, wrecking, there is little that can be proved; it was kept an even darker secret than smuggling, and tradition maintains an understandable silence about it. Incredibly, wrecking has become almost as popular a subject for story-telling as smuggling, though a more diabolical practice can hardly be imagined. There is only a vague and half-admitted tradition of wrecking in the Island, chiefly along its eastern coast. The shore at Ballure south of Ramsey has unspoken associations of this kind, which Hall Caine apparently knew of and used in one of his novels of Manx life. Two little boys playing on the shore decide that they will pretend to be wreckers like the terrible Carrasdhoo men they had heard of who,

> when the wind was rising in the nor-nor-west and there was a taste of brine on your lips, would be up and saying 'The sea's calling us, we must be going'. Then they would live in

rocky caves of the coast where nobody could reach them, and there would be fires lit at night in tar-barrels, and shouting and singing and carousing, and after that there would be ships' rudders and figure-heads and masts coming up with the tides, and sometimes dead bodies on the beach of sailors they had drowned.

In the days before there was a lighthouse at Maughold Head not far from Ballure, it was said that on stormy nights when the wind was inshore a lantern was set in the window of a house to lure ships onto the rocks, but people will say little about such things now, probably knowing very little and thinking them best forgotten.

Beyond Ramsey where the rocky headlands give way to sand-dunes, from Bride in the north right round to Jurby and Michael on the western coast, stories were once told of the band of villains known as the Carrasdhoo men, reputed to have been wreckers on the coast and robbers and murderers inland. They had a secret lair in the Jurby Curraghs where terrible deeds were done:

> There lay a hut by a lone wayside
> A publican's hovel, but woe betide
> The wretch whom thirst or weariness led,
> Into the dark pestiferous shed,
> For to drink there once was to drink no more
> And there came no tales from the dark trap door.

However one tale did come out, and these lines are from a poem in ballad style, based on an incident that happened in the early eighteenth century when an Irish pedlar boy called O'Dair was robbed and murdered, and his body was thrown into the bog. The murder was done in the ale-house where he was staying for the night, a *shebeen* in the curraghs, and at the time it must have horrified the whole countryside for the story became part of Jurby folklore. Esther Nelson, a local clergyman's daughter perpetuated the memory of it in verse, and in doing so cast a lastingly deeper shade over the Jurby curraghs with their sinister black pools among the sally willows. She rather improbably described the rank-growing wormwood as proliferating in the bogs, introducing it no doubt because she liked the sound of its Manx name, *Ullymar,*

a word that tolls in her poem like a knell for the murdered pedlar boy –
Ugh cha nee! for the youth that sleeps
down where the bitter Ullymar weeps!
Somehow her verses got back to the people – they would have made a dramatic item at a 'penny-reading' – and in one old person's reminiscence of the finding of the dead youth 'with his yellow hair all draggled in the mud' there wandered a strange phrase about 'the lone star of Ullymar' like a line from Edgar Allan Poe, that was in fact an imperfectly recollected memory of Esther Nelson's poem where she tells of a local belief that a certain star shone over the curraghs when the Carrasdhoo men were at work:

> There is a bright and fatal star
> That shines o'er the feathery Ullymar,
> And when that cold star hath height and power,
> Grim death is abroad, and fate hath her hour!

The murder of O'Dair cannot have been an isolated incident, there must have been other grim happenings of the kind and the bogs have swallowed up other victims beside the Carrasdhoo men's, but their crimes were the best remembered and the most celebrated:

> I rede ye beware of the Carrasdhoo men
> As ye come up the wold,
> Oh, I rede ye beware of the Curragh glen
> Be ye ever so brave and bold ...
> For the Ullymar bogs have a hideous slime,
> And the Ullymar bogs wear the hue of crime!

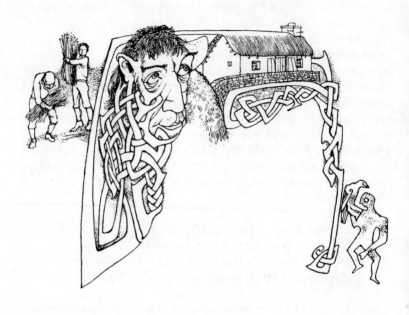

12 The Farmer and his Friends

THE SCIENCE OF AGRICULTURE was a mystery unknown to the earlier Manx farmer and crofter, and the cultivation of his land was a way of life, not a business run for profit. Agricultural improvers of the eighteenth century found much to complain of in the way he lived and worked. 'Agriculture is here yet a recent art', wrote one, 'the attention it receives from the numerous yeomanry, among whom the soil is principally divided is still deficient ... With models of improvement before their eyes ... this class of men slowly deviates from ancient practice.'

That was how it looked from the outside to the critical observer, but those living the life seemed to be scarcely aware of their shortcomings. Edward Faragher described the life of the Cregneash people in the nineteenth century:

No doubt the old people of Cregneash were not like some others of their neighbours in the little sea-port town, with their *perree-bane* (short white coat), *keeir-lheeah* (dark-grey) knee-breeches) and *carranes* (hide shoes), but they were more innocent and kinder to one another; they all used to help one another to get the crops down, and in the harvest, helped each other to cut the corn and stack it ... There were only two farmers in Cregneash that had a pair of horses, but there were a good many of them that had one, and then two of them joined together at ploughing time. They had wooden ploughs in those days. I remember them very well, and one of the little farmers would be lending the plough to the other.

With this attitude to life, the money value of the work they did and the time spent in doing it mattered very little. The Manxman's supposed motto *'traa dy liooar',* 'time enough', is a misunderstood and misapplied saying, stigmatising him as lazy and shiftless, a reputation he earned when getting on and making money were considered the only worthwhile aims in life. This view point, which many have since come round to, was alien then, and they could even make a joke about their poverty, consoling themselves when times were worse than usual with the reflection that even though they had no money, there was 'gold on the cushags' (ragwort) still.

To balance this lack of worldly ambition there was much neighbourliness, as Edward Faragher remembered:

My aunt was talking about old times, the other day, in her youthful days in Cregneash. When the cows of one family were dry, the rest of the neighbours that had cows milking were dividing the milk with them that had none. I recollect myself when there was no paying for milk in Cregneash ... and a big vessel holding half a gallon standing on a dresser full of buttermilk ... was always kept full for anyone who was thirsty.

This mutually helpful habit of mind was an inborn characteristic, and rooted in an old economy in which there was much common ownership, and everyone had their part to play, and their share to contribute to the life of the community.

One of the greatest changes that has taken place in the Island is the loosening and almost final severance of the old social ties, and the withdrawal of the individual into his or her personal struggle to make a living. In the past work and leisure drew people together, so that participation in the life of the community was almost unavoidable. Large companies of people met together at work in the fields, at church and chapel on Sundays, and at the festivals throughout the year whose observation was everyone's concern: and at the parish fairs they gathered together and met friends and relatives from all parts of the Island.

Manners were more free and easy in those days, and so according to one account were ceremonial occasions. The writer describes what he saw at Tynwald fair or Midsummer Fair as it used to be called, to which the farming families of the whole Island went in their hundreds to see the Governor and other dignitaries take their places on the Hill, and to hear the laws read out to the assembled commons, but from his observation of their behaviour they seem to have been quite unimpressed by the importance of the occasion.

> The Tynwald Hill . . . had a small tent with red sides and white roof erected on its summit, and rushes strewn according to custom on the floor . . . I was doubtful of being suffered to trespass within the sacred wall of the hill; but lo! on approaching I found lots of people scrambling over and inside it sans ceremony, and on following their example, I discovered that the penetralia of the tent itself were not in the least taboo, nor even the faded red moreen thrones set apart for the Governor and the Bishop; for upon these, and on the side benches, were seated farmers and their wives, and masters of Peel herring smacks, joking about the dignity of their position, and saying how pleasant it was to be out of the sun!

A state of affairs that would not be tolerated today, though if the farmers or their wives or any others of the commonalty managed to seat themselves for a moment on the places on the Hill, there would still no doubt be joking about the 'dignity of position', but the joke might be a little less good-humoured than it was a century ago.

In the old days families stayed together and helped each

other, all working together to run a farm or croft, and the old people lived on in the family home when the son or the daughter took over the management of the farm or the house. Nothing else was thought of: the day of the institution had not dawned. There are some pathetic tales told of the mentally deranged being shut away in a room or an outhouse, even it is said sometimes chained to a wall. The poor and the indigent took to the road.

Nothing reflects more creditably on the character of the old Manx people than does their treatment of the beggars who came to their door. Up to the end of last century there was a drifting population who travelled about the Island at will, entirely accepted and taken for granted by its settled inhabitants. On some farms they built a special house for them to use, the *thie ny moght,* the house for the poor, though it was usually known as 'the beggars' house'. There were both men and women wanderers, though the women were fewer, who travelled round the country, and were given food and a seat by the fire and a bed at night. Where there was no beggars' house they slept in a barn.

It was inevitable that there should have been some rogues among them, like Mick Collins who once gathered a random handful of children off the Douglas streets and took them out to Kirk Lonan, where he called at the first farm he came to with a pitiful story of how he had just buried his wife, and had no money to pay for the funeral, or to buy food for the poor motherless children. The farmer and his wife were full of sympathy and brought them into the house and gave them the broth that had been prepared for their own dinner, which the children, hungry with their long walk soon made short work of; but Mick Collins, overcome with grief was hardly able to eat at all, and kept murmuring brokenly between mouthfuls, 'Six feet deep, yer honour, six feet deep!'.

Apart from one or two such rascals, these foot-loose wanderers were an eccentric, but on the whole a harmless company. Dan Nascoin was one who was never very welcome as he had a bitter tongue and rather unpleasant ways. Some were simple enough characters like the man who arrived one morning at a farm where corn was being threshed with a steam mill, and was persuaded by the men who were working it to go and ask the farmer for the job of 'wheeling smoke away'. Peter O'Clark must have presented the oddest appearance of any of them, as he wore several layers of tattered coats well secured about him with rope, to which in cold wet weather he was known sometimes to add a top layer of thatch. Little or no work was expected of them in return for the hospitality they were given, though a pair who called regularly at one farm used to stand at the door of the barn where they were to spend the night and sing a duet –

> Let the hurricane roar,
> It will the sooner be o'er

but whether this was intended as a thank-offering, or merely because they liked singing, no-one seemed to know. They were a strange company whose like will never be seen again. Their coming served one purpose; they brought the news and gossip from other parts of the Island in the days when news travelled slowly, which may have been one reason why they were made welcome.

This shifting population had certain other members who were less easily accounted for, though they had names which identified them to some extent; they were the *fynnoderee* and the *glashan* and the *dooinney oie* or night man. They were spoken of usually in the singular but in all probability were a fairly numerous tribe, and they must be numbered among the farmers' friends, as it was on the farms that they were most often to be found, though they were rarely seen, and they always seemed to be awaiting an opportunity to share in the work. Writers on folklore often include them among the fairies, but there was a substantial human quality about them, however much they were given to vanishing from sight when anyone appeared. They were shy and elusive so they came down from their lairs in the hills and from the glens at night to do their work secretly and unobserved, when they threshed the corn in the barns and attended to it in the little corn mills and in the drying kilns that were used on the farms many years ago. The *dooinney oie*, the night man was a real friend to the farmers, warning them of coming storms, and when they heard him blowing his horn, they knew it was time to get their sheep and cattle into shelter.

The best-known of them all was the fynnoderee, though he had a double on the southern side of the Island called the glashan about whom very similar stories are told. These names have never been satisfactorily explained, though a guess has been made at 'hairy stockings' for the fynnoderee, and the glashan is thought to have been a close relative of the Scottish *glaisig* a brownie. The fynnoderee had uncommon strength: he could carry great loads of stones, and once he cut two fields of corn for a farmer in the parish of Bride in one night. In fact reaping and mowing were skills at which he was adept, and one of the names by which he was known in Manx, *Yn Foldyr Gastey*, means the nimble mower. There are many stories about him, but his most notable exploit was once when he chased and caught a hare, and in so doing proved himself to be a bit of an *ommidan*, a fool.

There was a farmer who had a flock of sheep on the mountain, and one night when it was beginning to snow he went to bed very uneasy about them in his mind, wishing he had brought them down to shelter. Towards morning the storm grew worse, and unable to sleep he was thinking he might as well get up when he heard a voice calling to him from the window, 'Are you there mastha?, the sheep is all in at me now, but I had a terrible job with the *l'il loghtan* (little brown sheep); I had to chase him three times roun' Snaefell before I got him in with the res' '. When daylight came and the farmer went out to his sheepfold he found his flock all safe and sound, and in amongst them the *l'il loghtan* that had given the fynnoderee so much trouble, a brown mountain hare!

It is this story that gives a partial clue to the fynnoderee's identity, and proves that he had some very aristocratic connections among the heroes of Celtic and even of Norse legend: similar stories are told of Finn McCooil, and of Peredur in the Welsh Mabinogion – the Parzival of Grail Legend – and there are similarities too in the story of Sigurd of the Volsungs. The Manx fynnoderee was in one of his aspects a hero of ancient romance who had fallen on evil days, but he was more than that for he was an exceedingly composite creature who seems to have been personally burdened with the characteristics of every kind of fairy, troll, brownie, uruisg, and boggart that ever came to our shores. It is possible too that he was even once a human being – on one side of his ancestry – it was more than likely that he was in recollection a surviving remnant of an earlier race living in the wild and remote places of the Island, not altogether avoiding the people living in the farms, but shy and wary of them, and only venturing out at night. In romantic versions of his story, the fynnoderee is supposed to have been banished to the wilds because he failed to turn up in time at the revels at the court of the fairy king, and instead 'kept tryst with a Manx maiden'. This may be a touched up or played down version of the kind of behaviour to which his kind were said to be prone, the abduction of a child or young girl to their lair in the hills. It has to be said in all fairness to him that except in this romantic context, there is no hint of this kind of conduct in fynnoderee tradition, but his counterpart in the Scottish Highlands, the *uruisg,* a kind of wild savage living in remote corries, was certainly accused of it. John Buchan has written a story probably based on uruisg tradition, about a man who finds just such a remnant of an ancient people among the Scottish hills, who carried away little girls and killed sheep and lambs with flint arrow-heads.

If it is possible to entertain the possibility of a primitive survival of this kind, one wonders whether the fierce creatures of Buchan's imagining were nearer to the reality than the brownie and the boggart, Lob-lie-by-the-fire, and the other fairly genial manifestations of it in folklore, some of whom seem to have been half-domesticated, and the worst of them only mischievous, perhaps malicious, but not really vicious. The uruisg was clearly of a different breed, and in Buchan's story the country people lived in terror of their savages. There seems to have been little fear of the fynnoderee in the Isle of Man. Like the beggars, he was made welcome, and there was food left for him in the barn as a reward for the work he did, and it was by exceeding this hospitality and by over-charitableness that the farmers lost his services in the end.

The story is, and it is told in several parts of the Island, that pity was taken on his naked state (for he wore no clothes only a covering of shaggy hair), and a suit of clothes was left for him by a well-meaning farmer, which so offended him that he went away and never came back.

'Cap for the head, bad for the head,
Coat for the back, bad for the back',

he is supposed to have said on finding the clothes, 'If this glen is thine, merry Glen Rushen is not thine', and it was to

Glen Rushen he went to live, and was never seen around the farms again. Perhaps the people who long ago benefited from his shyly performed labours tried too hard to domesticate the wild man of the hills, if that was what he was, and frightened him away. If fear of him existed it has been forgotten: he seems to have been regarded almost with affection, for when he was gone, the old people used to say, 'There has never been a merry world since the fynnoderee lost his ground.'

13 Hollantide to Harvest

THE ISLE OF MAN is so small that in theory it would seem possible to trace the life of its people back to its beginnings in unbroken sequence, but though this might be done in the material sense, with folklore it is less likely. Traditions can be irrevocably lost along the way, or there can be failures and breaks in the transmission of them, which a mere collector of such material can never hope to make good. In the absence of written records, only oral tradition can provide an insight into the minds of early peoples, for archaeology, with its discoveries of how they lived and more especially of how they died and were buried, has been able to reveal only a little of what they believed.

Folk tradition which represents the collective memory of a people over many periods, the customs and ceremonies surrounding their daily life and work, once as important as the work itself and an integral part of it, cannot be ascribed with any certainty to a particular people or time. Yet farming has been known in the Island for thousands of years and it is not unreasonable to suppose that the traditions conncected with it are some of the oldest in Manx folklore. How far they can be traced into the distant past is impossible to guess; they could have had their beginnings anywhere along the way, but we do know that some of them have persisted almost into modern times, and that it is only comparatively recently that the many precautions taken to preserve cattle, especially milking cows and their produce from harm were generally abandoned, and it would be rash to assume that they have entirely ceased to be practised today.

The pagan powers that influenced our ancestors over the last few centuries were embodied in recognisable forms, in fairies, bugganes and spirits, and sometimes in actual persons, like witches and wizards and wise men and women of various degrees and kinds, and the many tales that are told about them seem as if they happened only yesterday. The folklore of farming and the festivals of the agricultural year are more deeply rooted in the past, in observances to gods who though nameless can sometimes be identified as those of Celt and Norseman, and further back still, in the veneration of natural objects, water, trees and hills, and of elemental forces and of the seasons, the sun and moon, light and darkness. A preoccupation with weather in all its aspects, and reaction to natural surroundings was and still is an inevitable characteristic of farming people. The many misfortunes to which a farmer is prone, the failure of crops and the disease and death of cattle, which were latterly regarded as the result of witchcraft and the evil eye, must originally have been attributed to inimical natural forces, which to primitive man were the most powerful and mysterious he knew. Out of them he created his gods.

At no time of year can they have been aware of these forces so strongly as towards the end, when, as winter came on, all they feared and stood most in awe of seemed to be closing in around them, while those powers that aided and favoured their existence were in retreat. It was in this dark season of the year, in November, at the onset of winter, that the Manx people like the rest of the Celtic world celebrated the New Year. The feast of Sauin, marking the end of summer, for that is what the word means, was one of the chief festivals in the Celtic calendar. Its date, the twelfth, changed with the new calendar like that of other festivals to the first of the month, is still one of the four Manx quarter days, the time of year when land and property are let and leased and rents are due. Hollantide Fair, immemorially held on this date has lapsed only recently, and was a hiring fair for farm workers. The season of Sauin was a fateful time in the farming year, heralding the change to winter conditions and concerned with the necessary preparations to meet them. With the prospect of cold weather and short days ahead, it was the time for bringing cattle in from the pastures to the safety and shelter of cowhouses and cattle-sheds where in the old days they stayed warm and protected until spring. There was a firm belief that the animals were threatened not only by the approach of bad weather, but by harm from the evil influences let loose upon the world at the season of Sauin, whose powers increased as the year declined into darkness.

Even when these beliefs were no longer held so strongly, there was a general feeling that it was better for livestock to be indoors, and the practice of housing them by the twelfth of November continued especially among older farmers, though it was carried out with less fanatical zeal. In the old days, Manx cowhouses had no windows, only ventilation slits which were kept firmly blocked up throughout the winter to exclude anything that might be harmful, whether draughts or evil spirits. The practice of taking cattle indoors by this date may have been grounded in superstitious belief, but there was plenty of practical justification for it. In those years when winter set in early, and the grass withered in the fields, there was little point in leaving them out where there was no grazing to be had. The superstitious basis for it need not be too contemptuously dismissed: before the identification and eradication of the more virulent cattle diseases, infected animals seldom survived the winter, or if they did, they died off in the spring. Farmers saw their stock becoming weak and dying off mysteriously, and in the absence of veterinary knowledge, it is no wonder that unknown powers of evil were suspected and blamed for their loss where the cause of death was never established. Even today people feel the need to find a reason for inexplicable misfortune, if ony for a spell of bad weather.

Before agriculture had advanced sufficiently to enable farmers to keep their cattle alive through the winter, the festival of Sauin possibly coincided and became associated with an enforced slaughter of cattle towards the end of the year. This is not remembered in the Isle of Man, but there is the recollection of a time when cattle kept through the winter were so weak from starvation that when spring came they had to be dragged or carried out into the open to graze. It became customary on Manx farms and crofts to kill a beast and salt it down at the beginning of winter. This was of course a more recent development, for pickled meat and fish became an important ingredient of the people's diet when salt could be obtained for curing. Salt is listed among the Island's imports in the sixteenth century and when it became generally procurable it earned a great reputation as an antidote against evil, and a preserver of much else beside carcases. In an early reference to it, a ship's crew from Ireland met on the coast of the Isle of Man 'a person who was every alternate year a maker of salt'. There is a Manx song of unknown though extreme age, deriving from a period possibly anterior to this rather sporadic salt manufacture, which mentions some of the practices associated with the season of Sauin or more particularly with the night preceding it, *Oie Houney*, Hollantide Eve. The words are obscure and in the main have baffled folklorists, but some of the more intelligible lines refer to the selection of an animal for killing, and the subsequent cooking and eating of it at the New Year feast of *Hop Tu Naa*. This phrase which recurs in the song as a refrain is generally considered to be a corrupt version of the Manx *Shoh ta'n Oie* (This is the Night) and Hop Tu Naa has now taken over as the name of the festival, and its old Gaelic name of Sauin is almost forgotten. It has been suggested that certain lines of the Hop Tu Naa song contain 'some reminiscence of sacrifice and feasting' rites that may once have been associated with the Celtic New Year Festival:

> *Shibber y gounee* – Supper of the heifer,
> *Cre'n gauin gow mayd?* – What heifer shall we take?
> *Yn gauin beg breck* – The little spotted heifer.

– lines which clearly promise a feast, but there is little reason to suppose that it was a sacrificial one.

Hop Tu Naa, as it is usually called, is one of the few old Celtic festivals that is still honoured by some kind of observance. Children go about from house to house after dark on Hollantide Eve carrying elaborately carved turnip lanterns, and singing a rather worn-down version of the old song of Oie Houney: 'Jinny the witch (or 'the squinney') went over the house, To get a stick to lather the mouse, Hop Tu Naa, Hop Tu Naa.' Held in the other hand of at least one of the band, and without doubt the main purpose of the evening, and the probable reason for the survival of the custom is a collecting tin for coppers. Added interest has been aroused in it in some junior schools by holding competitions for the best turnip lantern, so it would seem that turnip lanterns have achieved a popularity second only to that of corn dollies.

Some of the practices that formerly belonged to this night have been borrowed from it and attributed to the end of December and the January New Year. It was a time for prophesying, for weather prediction and fortune-telling. The ashes of the fire were smoothed out on the hearth last thing at night to receive the imprint of a foot. If next morning the track pointed towards the door, someone in the house would die, but an inward pointing footprint indicated a birth during the coming year. A cake was made on Hollantide Eve which was called the *Soddag Valloo,* or Dumb Cake, because it was made and eaten in silence. Young women and girls all had a hand in baking it on the red embers of the hearth, first helping to mix the ingredients, flour, eggs, eggshells, soot and salt, and to knead the dough. The cake was divided up and eaten in silence, then still without speaking, all who had eaten it went to bed, walking backwards, expecting and hoping to see their future husband in a dream or vision. A salt herring stolen from a neighbour and roasted on the fire in its salt brine and also eaten in silence served the same purpose, but if this way of fore-telling the future was resorted to, it was forbidden to have anything to drink, as the husband-to-be would, when he appeared in the dream, 'present a drink of water' – a realistic touch, as a herring cooked straight out of the pickle is so impregnated with salt as to be almost inedible, and would be calculated to produce a raging thirst which mere 'visionary water' would do little to quench.

Weather and its likely effect on their crops was never far from people's minds, and weather prediction in the old days was almost a profession. To the old Manx people November represented the first month of the winter and of the year, and the coming year's weather was predicted from its first twelve days, each day and its weather representing the month of the same number. This kind of weather forecasting is still practised in an idly speculative way, when people are reminded of the old custom by contrasting extremes of weather: a rarely sunny day will be found to correspond with November and a day of storm and blizzard will represent June. The reckoning now is usually made from the first twelve days of January, as the Celtic year is no longer observed, or more correctly as it is thought now from the fifth of January, which is Old Christmas Day.

The hardships of winter rarely made themselves felt until the turn of the year. The days shortened but the weather until the end of December, though often wet, was usually fairly mild. The long days of work through the first half of the year, from daylight to dark, had brought their reward, meagre enough in some years when the season had been a poor one, but enough to be going on with. The crops were gathered in and the stacks well-thatched in the haggart, the cattle housed and safe from harm and there was a sense of well-being and comfort. It is doubtful if there was actual leisure to be enjoyed, there were tasks waiting to be done, but they were of a kind that could be done indoors. The making and mending of fishing nets and other gear used at sea and at home was in itself a kind of leisure, and they used to say philosophically 'change of work is rest'. The women had plenty to occupy them. The year's wool crop had to be carded and spun ready for weaving, as all thread used in making clothes and furnishing was handspun at home. Spinning was not necessarily a winter occupation, it was done when required, but the long dark nights allowed more time for it, and it was besides a more auspicious time. There was a saying that *'Te foddy ny share ve snieu tra ta ny kirree cadley'* (It's far better to be spinning when the sheep are asleep'). A notion that was not confined to the Isle of Man; it appears also to have been a North Country belief. Wordsworth knew of it and wrote a spinning song based on it;

> Ply the pleasant labour, ply
> For the spindle while they sleep
> Runs with speed more smooth and fine . . .
> While the flocks are all at rest
> Sleeping on the mountain's breast.

It doesn't say so in the Isle of Man, but in 'the Pastoral Vales of Westmorland' the spinners spinning at night were aware of 'help as if from fairy power', though in an old Manx spinning song, a woman sings, *'Dy chooilley vanglane er y villey sneiu er-my-skyn'* ('Every leaf on the tree spin above my head'): there was obviously more than one source of help on which a spinning-woman could draw.

The Manx language has a special word for these winter night occupations, *arnane,* which means 'work done at night by candlelight', and until oil lamps came into use towards the end of last century they had first to provide their candlelight by which the work could be done. Farming people made tallow candles and used them sparingly. Those unable to do this gathered rushes, and made the rushlights of which there was an inferior kind, the watch light which gave the feeble glimmer of light that Gilbert White described as 'darkness visible'. We can scarcely imagine the gloom of their winter days, and the nights, with at best only a dim glow of light in the house, and out of doors total darkness. If, as folklorists say, people imagined at this time that the powers of evil were 'stalking about the world with more than usual pride and aggressiveness', they had plenty of justification for doing so. Darkness is a great stimulator of the imagination.

It was in January and February that the pinch of both cold and scarcity began to be felt, for this was still the very depth of winter with a late spring to look forward to. Even in mid-February winter was reckoned to be only half over and at Candlemas Day, the second of the month, half the year's supply of fodder and fuel should still remain in store: *'Laa'l Moirrey my Gainle, leih foddyr as leih aile.'* Mary's feast day of the candle, half fodder and half fire. This nice apportioning out of resources was obviously a counsel of perfection and after a poor harvest was impossible to put into practice. By the time these winter words were noted down, much of the urgency had probably gone out of them. Such sayings as this originated at times of great want and scarcity when herring and corn harvests failed, and there was famine in the land. It was with the memory of these experiences in mind that an almost obsessional watch was kept on the weather signs and conditions that would determine the season and the harvest to come.

Bad weather was looked for and often came in December

and January: 'Between St Thomas' Eve (21 December) and the Eve of St Bridget (1 February) lie two-thirds of all the storms of the year'. *Laa'l Breeshey Bane,* White St Bridget's Day, was anxiously awaited, as the weather on that day foretold the kind of spring weather to come. If it was a bright sunny day, there would be snow before May Day, but a wet morning foretold a fine spring. The weather lore of St Bridget's Day in inextricably mixed up with the activities of the *Caillagh ny Gueshag,* the Old Woman of the Spells, who at the beginning of February went out to gather dry sticks for her fire. She was also the *Caillagh ny Groamagh,* the Sullen Witch who was thrown into the Irish sea, and being a witch, didn't drown, but drifted towards the coast of the Isle of Man, and landing there one fine sunny February morning, set about gathering sticks to make a fire to dry herself by. The Caillagh tries to do this every year at the beginning of February and if she is able to get dry sticks for her fire, the spring is sure to be a wet one.

It was when the end of winter was almost in sight that people were most obsessed with weather prospects, and between the New Year and the end of April, the Manx calendar bristles with weather sayings. This was not because of winter's severity, for the Manx climate is a fairly equable one and extremes of weather are rare. Winters often pass without much snowfall, though it snows often enough to have established a few weather and other rules. 'If you get it before Christmas you won't get it after' and 'if Peel hill is covered with snow on Old New Year's Day there will be a good herring year'. The trouble about a Manx winter is its length. It drags on into unseasonable months: as in northern England 'spring comes slowly up this way' and often comes only in name. The many weather sayings of the end of winter are wrung from a hard experience of hungry months with the 'half fodder and half fire' long ago exhausted, and signs of spring as far away as ever. In January the testing day was *Laa'l Paul,* the 25th:

St Paul's Day stormy and windy,
Famine in the world and great death of mankind,
Paul's Day fair and clear,
Plenty of corn and meal in the world.

In March they looked for a breeze to dry the ground for sowing and planting:

Sheeu kishan dy yoan mayrnt maaill bleeaney Vannin.
A kishan of dust in March is worth the rent of the Isle of Man.

April supplied the severest test of all:

February will feel, March will try, and April will tell whether you'll live or die.

No Manx farmer needed or needs to be told that April is the cruellest month; he knew, and knows it only too well. He had another name for it – the hungry month. Often the drying winds that should have come in March blew harsh and cold in April, blasting the young grass. Weariness of winter and longing for warmth and sunshine find expression in words that are like a long sigh, *Cha beayn as y lomman arree* ('As lasting as the parching winds of Spring'). Even those in more recent times who never knew the privations their ancestors endured, would tend to look at their bare fields and emptying haggards in early spring, and say 'It's a long time 'til the twelfth of May'.

From the very earliest days, the Month of May must have been a time of complete renewal to farming people, the long-hoped-for release from the grip of winter. It meant the beginning of a new growing season, when half-starved animals could graze again in the fields, and it brought the promise of increasing strength and warmth of sunlight, fresh budding of trees and blooming of flowers. It was the Celtic Beltain, the festival of Spring, celebrated with a ritual gathering and strewing of the first plants and flowers of the season, symbols of the rebirth of life and power in all growing things. On the Eve of May Day, green branches and yellow flowers were gathered and spread around the doors and windows of dwelling-houses and cattle-sheds; branches of tramman (elder) were hung up and the twigs of the mountain ash were made into crosses, the *crosh cuirn,* and placed over doorways and hidden in the long hair of the tails of cattle to protect them from harm. The yellow flowers of spring were the most potent to combat harm from witchcraft, and to ward off the influences of the evil eye. Primroses, the commonest of them were usually gathered on May Eve: 'we would be goin' down the 'lion (glen) to get primroses to put round the door', the old people used to say.

But it was the King Cup or Marsh Marigold that was most sought after as a source of protection against witches. One of its Manx names was *Lus y Voaldyn,* the Herb of Beltain or May (though it was commonly called the *blughtan*), and as it was essential that it should be among the flowers gathered on May Eve, the first signs of its flowering or 'breaking' were anxiously looked for. A farmer in Kirk German, who kept a diary over a number of years in the late eighteenth century, noted down the breaking of the blughtan each spring. Sometimes it was late, and there was a growing note of anxiety in his April entries: 'The blughtan not broke yet.' 'No sign of the blughtan breaking.' Then at last, almost at the end of the month, 'The blughtan broke' – but only just in time for its flowers like small golden suns to add their brilliance to the May rites. Yellow flowers and green branches were the farmer's safeguards against the power of witches who with a sweep of the arms and a few muttered words could draw to themselves the *tharrey,* the whole profit of his cattle and his dairy and crops, and blast his fields and his herds with infertility. Flowers and fire were the chief features of the ritual of Beltain, for the people set fire to the gorse on the hills and on the field hedges 'to burn out the witches', and the smoke blew over the fields and purified them, and they drove their cattle between the fires. When the gorse fires were all blazing and the hedges alight, the hillsides seemed to be criss-crossed with 'walls of fire', and to add further terror to the scene, *dollans,* skin-drums, were beaten and horns blown all through the night 'to drive away the bad spirits'. When all these rites had been observed, and no precaution omitted, 'then the fields were ready to put the cattle on the grass'.

Corn-growing in the Isle of Man had a start of thousands of years over other crops, most of which came a long way after. A pottery sherd, with the imprint on it of a grain of wheat, was found on a Neolithic site on the Meayll Hill in Rushen, which means that wheat may have been grown here something like four thousand years ago. In historic times far more oats and barley were grown for bread, as much of the land was unsuitable for wheat. Grass and root crops came along eventually, and were grown and harvested with equal care, but their gathering in was far less of an event than the corn harvest. To the people of the Island 'the harvest' meant the grain harvest; hay was 'saved', usually in a wet midsummer, which might account for the use of the term, and potatoes were 'dug' or merely 'picked'.

The ancient traditions that surrounded the growing of corn could not be expected to survive the introduction of mowing machines, reapers and binders, and that final destroyer of the communally-based traditions of farming, the combine-harvester; and the 'taking of the *mheillea*', when the last sheaf was cut, has long been a thing of the past. Once it was the culminating moment of the harvest. The shearers – for in the old days corn was shorn, not cut – worked in twos side by side, advancing along the butt or strip of standing corn, shearing with their sickles as they went. Behind them came the band-makers, women or often children, tying handfuls taken from the swathes into bands which were laid on the ground ready for the lifters who followed behind, gathering up the swathes and tying them into sheaves. In a large cornfield there might be a dozen or more people, working the corn butts systematically until the field was almost finished. Then if it was the last field to be cut on the farm, the *mheillea* was taken; the final swathe of corn that had been left standing was ceremoniously cut by one of the young women reapers, and she made from it the *Babban ny mheillea,* the harvest baby or doll. This is how William Kennish remembered it in his own part of the Island round the middle of last century:

> Then Kitty, eldest of the youthful band
> Of females, challenged all within the field
> To be the first to cut with friendly hand
> The last oat sheaf the farm that year did yield;
> To form the 'Maiden' in its usual style
> With ribbon-bows and plaited straw-made arms . . .
> She bore it forth in triumph in her hand,
> Leading the shearers to the highest ground,
> Where met the rural and the happy band
> Whose hearty cheers did through the air resound:

This outcry of the reapers at the felling of the last of the corn was not merely a natural outburst of rejoicing because the work was finished –'Hurrahing in Harvest' in Gerard Manley

Hopkins' phrase – however reasonable it might be to suppose that it was. It was done the world over, or almost, wherever grain was grown, and its spirit, corn-spirit or rice-spirit, for that is what the last sheaf and the corn doll in its many forms is said to represent, could be caught, or killed, or driven into the barn.

Whatever it symbolised it was a custom that died out only gradually, lingering on in unexpected places. It was no surprise to see a few years ago a handful of corn hanging above the fireplace of a farm, not as might be expected hidden away among the hills, but on the outskirts of Douglas, and to hear of a last sheaf being quietly rescued from a binder and put away unobtrusively but safely in the barn. Only someone more than usually determined that 'custom' shall not 'weep' would attempt to salvage anything from the maw of a combine-harvester. It can only be hoped that in the harvest field today the 'corn-spirit' makes its escape and is saved without human assistance.

The current popularity of the corn-dolly doesn't signify any resuscitation of the old custom. Interest in it is not so much in the symbol itself as in the craft of making it, and is engendered not among farmers but here as elsewhere by Women's Institutes. It is doubtful whether harvest dollies in their more elaborate form even belong to the Island's harvest traditions; it is a custom that would have been much more likely to develop in the rich corn-growing counties of England, and though it may have been brought here and adopted on the fertile lowland farms around Castletown and beyond Ramsey, where wheat was grown, it is hard to imagine the Manx crofter cutting his oats and barley in small late-ripening fields near the hills, crowning his effort with elaborately wrought straw ornaments. However, rush-plaiting in a very similar manner was commonly done here in making toys for children.

Harvest in the Isle of Man is in fact often something of an anti-climax, and for some a disaster. The gathering in of a bountiful crop under the mellow skies of late summer is only a very occasional occurrence. In a wet season the lateness of the corn-harvest can be phenomenal. In the pre-combine days it wasn't unusual for stooks to be standing out in the fields, while, Sunday by Sunday, Harvest Thanksgiving Services were being held in Churches and Chapels all over the Island. In such conditions the harvest hymns would be adapted to suit the realities of the situation, the parson compromising with 'All will soon be gathered in'. There used to be another version of this hymn in popular circulation which was never sung in any church:

> All is safely gathered in
> All exceptin' ... ...
> His is still as green as grass,
> Then comes ... ... the las'.

Of the two late harvesters indicated, one probably farmed somewhere up at the mountain foot where harvests could be any time up to Christmas, and the other was possibly a firm believer in *traa dy liooar,* 'time enough'.

Bound up with the harvest, but very much more submerged in the people's memory was *Laa Luanys,* or Lammas Day. They observed it without realising that they were doing so or that such a festival existed, since all that remained of its ritual was a general inclination to climb to the tops of mountains on the first Sunday in August and visit any wells that could be taken in on the way. It cannot be said that in the Lammas Day celebration there were none of the witch-scaring, evil-dissipating performances of the other quarter day customs – they always seem to have been necessary. But very little is known of how the day was spent originally, as one of the few surviving accounts of its rites only tells how the inhabitants of Kirk Lonan climbed to the top of Snaefell, and behaved there 'very rudely and indecently'. The church disapproved strongly of the way the day was observed, and to give it holier associations the holiday was changed from the first of August to the first Sunday of the month. It is said that a Methodist preacher put a stop to the hill-top rites far more effectively than the Church's prohibitions had ever done, by taking a collection at a religious service held at one of these assemblies on the top of Snaefell. In its last phases, the custom became little more than an outing to the hills on a fine Sunday in August 'to gather blaeberries'.

Originally Laa Luanys was the day of Lugh, the Celtic god, who it is said, spent his boyhood in the Isle of Man as Manannan's foster-son. He was in the description of him in Irish records a brilliant figure: 'Like to the setting sun was the splendour of his countenance . . . they were not able to look in his face for the greatness of its splendour', from which it has been concluded that he was thought of as a sun god.

The celebration of this festival in Celtic myth has been interpreted as a contest between Lugh and a more primitive agricultural god called Crom Dubh who was a corn-bringer and cultivator and a ruler of the elements, from whom the young god Lugh of superior power and skill 'won the corn' for the benefit of the people. In the Irish legends surrounding the festival, St Patrick came to be substituted for Lugh, and it has been suggested that this happened also in the Manx folklore of Laa Luanys, and that the legends of the landing in the Island both of St Patrick and St Maughold may derive from the myths that are associated with this festival of harvest. To suggest such an origin is to introduce a heresy, as the legends of these saints are among the best known and most cherished Manx Christian traditions.

The visiting of wells was a great feature of Laa Luanys, and there are many 'holy' wells in the Island that before they acquired the names of Christian saints, Maughold, Bridget, Mary, Patrick and others, must have been the habitation of often malevolent water spirits that were venerated, feared and placated with offerings by the earlier peoples. The waters of the Island were the homes of creatures of several kinds, the *glashtin*, a water-horse that would descend with its rider into the depths of a watery world, the water-bull, the *Tarroo-Ushtey*, that lived in swamps and shallower pools, and sometimes roamed in the fields among the farm-cattle, and, not least, the dreaded *Nikyr*, a water-demon brought here from the swift-flowing rivers of the Norsemen, that found a very localised home in the deep and supposedly bottomless dubs or pools on the mountain streams that flow through and around some of the Norse-named upland treens of Kirk Lonan. Farms in this neighbourhood have names like *Brundalr*, spring dale, and in Gaelic, *Ballaglass*, river farm, for this was a very watery locality indeed, and a fitting home for a river god. The Nikyr's reputation lives on in the name of the water dubs on these rivers – Nikissen, the Nikyr's river. The legend of the child from a farm in Baldhoon who was lured into the depths of Nikissen is by no means forgotten in the valley to which it belongs, nor will be as long as the name of the pool persists.

The old rag and pin wells that were visited for cures probably represent a dual tradition, the pagan offering of a pin dropped in the well, or a bit of clothing left on a nearby bush, and at the same time, an invocation of distinctly Christian character. *Chibbyr Beltain* in Rushen is an instance, a well that from its name, Well of Beltain, had associations with the festival of Spring, and was visited 'for cures and for misfortune', and as the water was taken, a rag was left by the wellside 'as a return', that is in gratitude, and the water 'was lifted in the name of God, the Son and Holy Ghost'. Wells could be more readily Christianized than rivers, which is perhaps why the Nikissen legend has persisted. It is not unlikely that well-worship accompanied some of the other agricultural festivals, and under Christian influence, the 'holy' well became separated from its pagan associations.

The contest between the two harvest gods in some of the Irish legends took the form of a struggle for possession of a woman 'the pagan's daughter' and this helps to make sense of an apparent irrelevance in Manx Laa Luanys tradition which maintained that the day was kept in remembrance of Jephtha's daughter. People used to say that they climbed the hills in her memory, while others sat at home on the day reading the passage in the Bible about her wandering on the mountain tops. As St Patrick took the place of Lugh, Jephtha's daughter became in the Isle of Man the Christian substitute for the woman for whom the gods contended. In one of the Irish legends she was called Eithne, a name that means 'grain' or 'kernel' and it is thought that the woman may originally have been the personification of the corn.

Something like this may well have been the basis of the custom, but of its original significance the people latterly knew nothing: though as they made their annual pilgrimage on a fine August day to the tops of the mountains, they must have felt much the same as those earlier inhabitants of the Island who first observed Lugh's day, and knowing why they did so, climbed through the heather to the top of Barrule or Snaefell. Looking down they would have seen their farmland at the mountain foot; the green of the grass where the cattle grazed and the cornland turning to gold, a sight that might well have moved them to reverence for whatever power had brought it about. It was for this they had striven throughout the year in their daily work, and in the seasonal rites duly performed. It was the climax of the season, a short moment of perfection, as such a day in August can still be, when the harvest stands ready and waiting to be gathered, before the year declines into over-ripeness and decay.

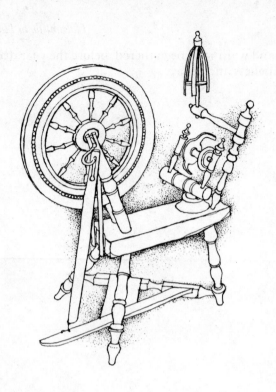

14 Old Christmas and the Oie'l Voirrey

IT CANNOT BE SAID that the people relinquished their old customs without a struggle, and some of the Christmas customs they held onto with something more than their usual tenacity, for it is was these that met with the greatest opposition. For this Methodism was largely responsible, an institution that combined a great influence on the life of the Island with an almost complete lack of understanding of and disregard for its traditions. Where it gained a hold, native Manx culture tended to disappear.

The early Wesleyans disapproved of the age-old amusements of music and dancing in which the people delighted. They found the language a stumbling block; they couldn't understand it and were uncertain of what their congregations were up to when they used it in the services.

Hymns in Manx were highly suspect (they had to undergo an examination before they were 'admitted to public use' even in translation). Of a proposal to publish a Manx hymbook John Wesley said: 'I exceedingly disapprove of publishing anything in the Manx language. On the contrary, we should do everything in our power to abolish it from the earth.' The Wesleyans provided another culture in place of what they destroyed, which in its turn became almost 'traditional', but it was at the expense of the Gaelic culture they found when they came here. Their antagonism to local custom showed itself in their determined effort to rid themselves of the *Oie'l Voirrey,* the service that was held in the Parish Churches on Christmas Eve, the Eve of the Feast of Mary, which is the meaning of the Manx name of the service; and especially to discourage the Carval-singing that went on at them. An attempt was obviously being made by the people to introduce the Oie'l Voirrey into the Methodist chapels, and official reaction to the move is recorded in a Minute Book dating from 1780, from which it is obvious that the congregations' addiction to the Oie'l Voirrey continued to plague the Methodist hierarchy for forty years. They never in fact succeeded in suppressing it.

The Christmas Eve service had always been a very special occasion in the Island, with the parish churches lit at night with candles that the people themselves provided, and decorated with evergreens, *hibbin as hollan,* ivy and holly. After a prayer had been said and a hymn sung, the parson went home and left the people to conduct the Oie'l Voirrey in their own way, under the supervision of the parish clerk who saw that all was done in a seemly manner. The great feature of the service and its main purpose was the singing of *Carvals,* carols, which were however totally unlike English Christmas carols. A few were on the subject of the nativity or mentioned the birth of Christ and events in His life, but in the main they were long rambling poems in the Manx language composed by the people themselves, many of them on the themes of sin and repentance, death and judgement, and the torments of hell. Some dealt with Biblical events and persons, like the *Carval ny Drogh Vraane,* the Carol of the Bad Women, which reviewed the careers of some of the wicked women mentioned in the Scriptures. The fall of Adam, the conversion of St Paul, and the sinful cities of Sodom and Gomorrah were subjects that also appealed to the Carval-writers. But whatever their theme at the outset, the punishment of sin and the need for repentance were sure to appear before the end. There were some in which the day of judgement and the resurrection of the dead were visualised with awful clarity:

> I quaked to see the dead arise,
> A sight too strange for mortal eyes,
> In rank on rank they rose and spread,
> Innumerable crowds of dead.

They were obsessed with the thought of the fires of hell that awaited unrepentant sinners, in which they burned but did not die:

> The fire that ne'er extinguished is,
> But will for ever burn,
> Wherein they unconsumed are burn'd
> Each mortal in his turn.

The length of the Carvals was extraordinary, thirty or forty verses, throughout which the writer and subsequently the singer laid bare his sinful soul, for they were sung as solos or by two singers taking alternate verses. The pair would stand with candle in hand to light their carval book, at the west end of the church, advancing a pace or two after the singing of each verse, so that even the longest carval was finished by the time they stood before the altar. When hours later the carval singing was over, the tone of the Oie'l Voirrey lightened considerably, and it was customary for the young women present to bombard their bachelor friends with parched peas which they had brought for the purpose. Then as on other occasions the company adjourned to the ale-house, to drink Manx home-brewed ale spiced with pepper, until the long Christmas candle had burned down in its socket, and it was time to sing the *Arrane Oie-Vie*, The Good-Night Song, which reminded them that 'blackness had come on the chiollagh' and that the very chairs they sat on were urging them to go home to bed.

It is probable that the Manx Carval writers were no more preoccupied with hell and its torments than others of their day who believed in them, but they let their imaginations dwell on them in graphic detail. In the *Carval of the Godly Man's Vision*

(many of the sightings of hell were obtained in visions) the
gates are seen closing on the damned:

> The gates of hell were very strong and very wide and high
> They open'd in the middle part, and turn'd on either side,
> And every time they open'd them, wide open they were put,
> And very many thousands thus within by them were shut.

Most of the carvals were probably written in the eighteenth
century but some may be older. One of the most interesting is
on the mediaeval theme of a dispute between body and soul. A
soul is seen in a vision escaping out of hell pursued by fiends,
and going to sit by the open grave where its former body lies,
where it upbraids it for its share in the sins of their past life
which brought the soul to its present plight;

> O, mouldering body, earth and dust,
> Little dost thou know where thou art lying,
> What heavy torment I am left in:

The body acknowledges its share of blame, but asks in turn
why the soul did not attempt to restrain it instead of
consenting to the sins they committed together.

One cannot help wondering reading these carvals how the
Wesleyans ever came to accuse the people of an addiction to
'levity'. There are one or two of a less lugubrious nature which
give glimpses of the lighter side of Christmas: the brightly lit
church on the night of the Oie'l Voirrey:

> It is a heavenly sight to see
> In the darkness of the night,
> The congregation praising God
> Their candles burning bright.

– and the games and amusements, the dancing and fiddling
that accompanied Christmas throughout all its twelve days:

> "With eating and drinking, and 'choosing the leggads' "
> (valentines or partners for the coming year)
> Thus will we keep the feast . . .
> With the music of fiddles and with card-playing
> We would spend each night.

This is the kind of Christmas celebration Waldron described: 'There is not a barn unoccupied for the whole twelve days, every parish hiring fiddlers at the public charge; and all the youth, nay sometimes people well advanced in years making no scruple to be among these nocturnal revellers'. It is hard to believe that these 'revellers' could have been the same people who began the Christmas season by confessing themselves to be such woeful sinners at the Oie'l Voirrey.

In the end it became accepted in the chapels. The church's hold on the people weakened, and Methodism gained ground, and the Oie'l Voirrey moved from the church into the chapels especially the smaller ones in the country, which in their day were the main centres of social life for many people, with their tea-parties, concerts, anniversary and harvest services, and social gatherings throughout the year, among which the Oie'l Voirrey found a place. Its nature changed, and it was shorn of its trimmings of pea-shooting and ale-drinking and the 'disorderly work' so much objected to by the Wesleyans. Its date became more variable though it was still held in the Christmas season, but the numbers of the carval-singers diminished and the carvals themselves died out, to be replaced by hymn-singing, though still sometimes in Gaelic. In this greatly modified form, the Oie'l Voirrey lived on; in the little chapel of Kerrowkeil it has survived until the present day, and there are occasional revivals of it elsewhere.

There was one Christmas custom, that, however innocuous it later became (and it has not died out even yet), must have been very brutal in its original performance, the Hunting of the Wren on St Stephen's day, 26 December, when boys and men went out armed with sticks to beat the hedges and catch and kill the poor birds that were required for the carrying out of the wren ceremony.

The church disapproved probably of the whole custom, but certainly of the killing of the wrens, and though they continued to be hunted and killed even into the nineteenth century, in the later stages the performers dispensed with the necessity of providing a dead wren as a centre piece. The Hunt the Wren survived in the Island into the 1920s and '30s, even later in some places, and it is still done by children in Peel and occasionally in other parts. Formerly it was young men who went round, in groups of two or three, carrying their 'Hunt the Wren', two wooden hoops set at right angles to each other on top of a pole, and decorated with coloured streamers and evergreens. At every house where they called, they set the pole on the ground, and sang the Hunt the Wren song, and if they were lucky received some money in return.

> We'll hunt the wren, says Robbin the Bobbin,
> We'll hunt the wren, says Richie the Robin,
> We'll hunt the wren, says Jack o' the Lan'
> We'll hunt the wren, says everyone.

This was the formula for each verse, a repetition of the first line by each of the characters named, and as the song went on, the list of equipment needed to catch, kill, carry and cook the little wren grew more disproportionate to its size with every verse: 'the brewer's big cart' to carry him home, 'the brewery pan' to boil him in, 'a long pitch-fork' to lift him out and so on.

The custom has long lost its original significance, but in the eighteenth century it still meant something.

> On the 24th of December towards evening all the servants in general have a holiday. They go not to bed at night but ramble about till the bells ring in all the churches which is at 12 o'clock: prayers being over they go to hunt the wren and after having found one of these poor birds, they kill her and lay her on a bier with the utmost solemnity bringing her to the parish church and burying her with a whimsical kind of solemnity, saying dirges over her in the Manks language which they call her knell.

According to this wren-hunting took place on Christmas morning, but in more recent accounts it was on the following day that it was done, and there is some idea that it commemorated the martydom of St Stephen, whose day it was, *Laa'l Steaoin*, the Feast of St Stephen. There are various other explanations of the custom: that it is an act of revenge, because a wren betrayed the presence of the Manx Fencibles when they were in Ireland in 1798 by tapping on their drum, or in a totally different context because the wren is a re-incarnation of an enchantress who long ago lured the men of the Island into the sea and drowned them, then evaded capture by flying away as a wren: as a punishment she is doomed to re-appear each year in this form and be pursued and killed. Formerly it was customary to pluck the wren before burying it, and distribute its feathers for luck. In origin the Hunt the Wren may be related to the performances of the Christmas mummers, the White Boys, and the *Mollag Band,* who were essentially also purveyors of good luck and prosperity. One theorist, convinced of it antiquity, suggests that 'the wren cult reached the British Isles during the Bronze Age, and was carried by the Megalith builders', which, if it could be proved, would make it possibly the oldest surviving custom in existence.

Older generations of people in the Island held obstinately to the old date of Christmas day, for though with the change in the calendar they accepted the advancement of most of the other festival dates, they were reluctant to do so where Christmas was concerned, and made bewildering distinction between 'big' and 'little' and 'old' and 'new' Christmas day. For them *Shenn Laa Nollick,* Old Christmas Day, on 5 January was the 'real Christmas'. They felt very strongly about this and it almost seems as if some of the Christmas stories have been told and kept in memory simply because they proved them to be right.

A woman who had accepted the new way of thinking and kept Christmas on 25 December, decided that she and her servant girl would do some spinning on the eve of Old Christmas Day. They set to work, the girl very unwillingly as she was convinced they were doing wrong, but her mistress would not listen to her. They had not been spinning very long when the flax the mistress had on her wheel started to turn black, though the servant-girl's showed no change of colour. The spinning-wheels were put away at once, for this was proof enough that even the inanimate things of nature not only knew that this was the true Christmas eve, but could discriminate between the guilty and the innocent when pointing it out to be so.

The surest test of all was to watch at midnight on old Christmas eve to see whether the myrrh would flower. Myrrh used to be growing in almost every garden in the old days: it wasn't really myrrh, but Sweet Cicely, an aromatic plant, smelling and tasting of aniseed, and known everywhere in the Island as 'the myrrh'. At twelve o'clock on old Christmas eve people took a lantern and went out into the garden to see whether it had come up. It was often necessary to go out more than once to watch for it, but if you were lucky, you were eventually rewarded by the sight of the little greenish-grey shoot breaking above ground, which would burst into bloom for an hour or so, then disappear. 'We were always going out on Christmas eve to watch for the myrrh', the old people used to say, and it was only on Old Christmas eve that it would be seen, just as it was on that night that the bullocks, who like other creatures knew which was the true Christmas, went down on their knees, and the bees roused themselves and flew about the hive.

The controversy about the myrrh defies any final settlement: every year it is renewed and the question is asked 'is it really true that the myrrh breaks into flower on Old Christmas Eve? Have you ever seen it?' and some say they have and some say they haven't. The belief in it, or at least the hope that it may be true obstinately refuses to die, in spite of the pooh-poohing of the botanists who contend that 'it would come up anyway in a mild winter'. What they don't seem to have grasped is that it comes up and flowers for an hour – then disappears! After all there would be little point in making a midnight sortie by lantern-light on a cold January night if it were possible to see the plant flourishing next day in broad daylight. Sometimes the newspapers give the old custom an airing and publish a rather ghostly-looking picture of 'the myrrh in flower' in so and so's garden, and even apart from such publicity, it is pretty certain each year that there will be somebody going out to look for it.

15 Postscript

Some of the superstitions pronounced moribund in the 1890s have proved unexpectedly tenacious of life, which suggests that the imminent mortality or otherwise of customs and beliefs is a matter hard to determine. Those that have to do with growing things like the myrrh may have some advantage over abstract beliefs. The mountain ash springs afresh each year, and the *blughtan* 'breaks' in the bogs, and people can still gather them, and make the *crosh cuirn* to hang above the door, while the *tramman* grows ubiquitously and is still thought of as the fairy tree.

There are certain attitudes that have been just as persistent, and even today it is possible to come across the same ignorance of tradition as existed hundreds of years ago, and in the same quarter. Only recently a young Methodist preacher talking to the Sunday School children, told how he had cut down a tree that was darkening his study window, and urged them to take similarly drastic action with whatever was darkening their lives and obstructing the light of heaven. He had brought the stump along to show them and as he unwrapped it, there were some among his congregation who were quietly appalled to see that the tree he had cut down and wrapped in newspaper for an object lesson, was a tramman. One even went so far as to warn him afterwards that he'd better watch out or 'the fairies would have him'.

This was at least paying lip-service to the beliefs of the old people. We'd probably do well to go further and pay attention to the attitudes that inspired their creed, and perhaps even try to cultivate some of the best of them; their veneration for the natural world for instance, their response to it and obedience to its laws, which after all is what much of their folklore is about. In these things they were surely wiser than the people of today, and if we persist in thinking we know better now and have no need to acknowledge the gods the old people knew, we are probably deceiving ourselves, and it is more than likely that 'the fairies' the particular breed of them that wait to take revenge on those who refuse them recognition, will have us too in the end.

Such a reminder is scarcely necessary: people are only too well aware of where we are going wrong, and becoming more so, and as far as the Isle of Man's present predicament is concerned, will no doubt sit it out as former generations did in similar circumstances, *goll as gaccan,* as we say, 'going and grumbling'. As to the vexed question of the attitude to 'comeovers', it is enough to say that the people have never been unwelcoming to strangers in reasonable numbers and of a right-minded and well-disposed kind. To those who in all charity cannot be described as either, who come with grandiose schemes prepared to perform what are locally known as 'fates and fiddlesticks' the re-action by now is merely 'Aw well, we've seen them come, and we've seen them go", or more darkly *'Cha daink lesh y gheay nagh ragh lesh yn ushtey'* ('Nothing came with the wind that wouldn't go with the water') – which can be loosely paraphrased 'What blew noisily in is bound sooner or later to trickle ignominiously out, and like enough via the bankruptcy court'.

Meanwhile we can act on the advice of the old people who spoke out of experience of events of their time, and would have us believe that 'A wise man often makes a friend of his enemy', counsel worthy of the nodding and smiling seventh Earl of Derby himself, and for our private consolation when we feel ourselves to be slipping behind 'Maybe it's the las' dog that's catchin' the hare'.

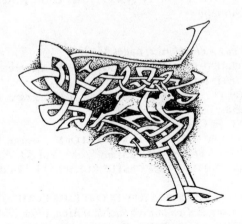

Notes

J.M.M.   *Journal of the Manx Museum*
I.O.M.N.H.A.S. *Isle of Man Natural History and Antiquarian Society*
Y.L.M.   *Yn Lioar Manninagh (The Manx Book)*
Fl.I.O.M.   *Folklore of the Isle of Man*
M.N.&Q.   *Manx Notes and Queries*

Introduction, pages 11–13
CELTIC ROUND HOUSES: Dr. Gerhard Bersu, *Celtic Homesteads in the Isle of Man, Journal of the Manx Museum.* V. 72-3, 1945-6, 177-82.
THE KINGDOM OF MAN AND THE ISLES: W. Cubbon and B. R. S. Megaw, *The Western Isles and the Growth of the Manx Parliament, Journal of the Manx Museum,* V, 66; 1942, 57-62.
ISLE OF MAN – A FOOTBALL: New Letters from T. E. Brown, *Mannin,* 9, 1917, 522.
SALE OF THE ISLAND TO WILLIAM LE SCROOP: John Parr, *An Abstract of the Laws. Customs and Ordinances of the Isle of Man,* I, 1867, *Manx Society,* Vol XII, 23.
SEVENTH EARL OF DERBY'S LETTER: Rev. W. Mackenzie, *Stanley Legislation in the Isle of Man,* 1860, 33, *Manx Society,* Vol. III.
Manx Folk Museum: Opened in 1938, the first publicly-owned Museum of its kind in the British Isles.
Maun: the earliest known version of the name of the Island, found inscribed on a tenth century Norse cross. Latin writer knew it as Mona and Monapia.

1   *The Folk and the Folklorists,* pages 15–25
LACK OF INTEREST IN MANX FOLKLORE: A. W. Moore, *Folklore of the Isle of Man,* 1891, Introduction, i, ii.
LEXICOGRAPHER: Archibald Cregeen, *A Dictionary of the Manx Language,* 1838.
FER–FEAYREE: A. Cregeen, op. cit. 66.
EARLIEST COLLECTOR OF MANX FOLKLORE: George Waldron, *A description of the Isle of Man,* 1726, *Manx Society,* Vol XI.
THE SPELL-BOUND GIANT OF CASTLE RUSHEN: G. Waldron, op. cit. 5, 6.
TRAVELLER GIVEN HOSPITALITY IN COTTAGE IN THE MOUNTAINS: David Robertson, *A Tour through the Isle of Man,* 1794, 75-8.
ROMAN CATHOLIC PRIESTS HARBOURED; ROMAN CATHOLIC CHILDREN IN SCHOOLS: G. Waldron, op. cit., 19, 20.

GEORGE BORROW'S VISIT: *Mannin*, II, 4, 1914, 201-9.
HIS JOURNEY TO THE HOUSE OF MYLECHARANE: *Yn Lioar Manninagh*. I. 1889, 359, 360.
TITLE OF HIS PROPOSED BOOK: *Journal of the Manx Museum*, IV, 59, 116.
MYLECHARANE BALLAD: A. W. Moore, *Manx Ballads and Music*, 1896, Words 52, Tune 254, (Discussion of the song in *Journal of Folk Song Society* VII, 28, 1924, 125).
VISIT OF J. F. CAMPBELL: A. W. Moore, op. cit., 1891, Introduction, i.
CHARLES ROEDER: *Contributions to the Folklore of the Isle of Man*, *Y. L. M.*, III, 1896, 129, 130.
ROEDER'S CORRESPONDENCE WITH EDWARD FARAGHER: *J.M.M.*, VII, 83, 1967, 39, 40.
THE CHARACTERS OF T. E. BROWN: *The Collected Poems of T. E. Brown*, 1901.

2   *The Fairy Belief*, pages 26–40

BUGGANE, FYNNODEREE, and FAIRIES: Current tradition in the Island.
FAIRIES TAKING: From personal knowledge.
UNICORN: H. R. Jenkinson, *A Smaller Practical Guide to the Isle of Man*, 1878, 106.
WOLF, GOAT: Charles Roeder, *Manx Notes and Queries*, 1904, 61, 67.
PURR MOOAR: W. W. Gill, *A Manx Scrapbook*, 1929, 272.
HUNCHBACK SHOEMAKERS: Sophia Morrison, *Manx Fairy Tales*, 1929, 60-5.
MANX PROVERB, 'IF' CUSTOM, ETC: Archibald Cregeen, *A Dictionary of the Manx Language*, 1838, 45.
ODIN IN MANX FOLKLORE: P.M.C. Kermode, *Traces of the Norse Mythology in the Isle of Man*, *Y.L.M.*, II, 1901, 38-154.
FAIRIES SUMMONED: Story told personally to author, around the 1930s.
CHA VEL AYRN ERBEE AYM AYNS CHREEST: *William Cashen's Manx Folklore*, 1912, 18.
ATTEMPTED ABDUCTION BY FAIRIES: *Y.L.M.*, II, 1901, 197.
CHARACTERISTICS OF FAIRY CHANGELING: George Waldron, *A Description of the Isle of Man*, 1726, 29, 31.
MANX-GAELIC AND DIALECT NAMES FOR FAIRIES; FAIRY PLACE NAMES: W. W. Gill, *A Second Manx Scrapbook*, 1932, 217, 220, 222.
POEM; THE CALLING OF THE NAME: 'Cushag' in Josephine Kermode, *Poems*, 1912, 70.
THE LAZY WIFE: Sophia Morrison, op. cit. 1929, 66.
FAIRIES: SIZE AND APPEARANCE, SPORTING IN THE TREES, FAIRY MAN SEEN: Charles Roeder, *Manx Notes and Queries*, 53, 54.
FAIRY TREE: *Yn Lioar Manninagh*, III, 1902, 152, 153; *M.N.&Q.* 1904, 53; Hall Caine, *The Deemster*, 1888, 263.

FAIRIES MARCHING: Sophia Morrison, op. cit. 60.

WOMAN IN FAIRY BATTLE: A. W. Moore, *Further Notes on Manx Folklore; Antiquary,* **XXXI**, 1895, 177.

FAIRIES RELUCTANT TO CROSS WATER: J. Clague, *Manx Reminiscences,* 1911, 169.

WATER FIGHT AT SANTON BURN: *Proceedings, I.O.M.N.H.A.S.,* 1933-34, 52.

BATTLE AT BALLGLONNEY BRIDGE: S. Morrison, *A Peel History Book,* Manx Museum M.S. No. 5433.

FAIRY HORSES AND RIDERS: PLOUGHMEN GOING TO FAIRY HOUSE: C. Roeder, *Y.L.M.* III, 146, 150, 160.

FAIRY MUSIC: Heard in stream – from oral source; Fairy fiddlers, *Y.L.M.,* I, 1889, 326. Donagher Lowey, *Y.L.M.,* III, 1902, 145.

PREPARATION FOR FEAST: Joseph Train, *History of the Isle of Man,* 1845, II, 164, 165.

FAIRY MUSIC HEARD BY HORSEMAN: G. Waldron, op. cit. 37; Sailor and hunting horn; idem, 33.

FAIRY TUNE – BILL PHERIC: *Y.L.M.,* II, 1901, 195; Travellers carried to edge of cliff: *Y.L.M.* III, 153.

STORIES OF FAIRIES' DEPARTURE: Jurby farmer, *Y.L.M.* I, 327.

'HEY FOR IRELAND': J. W. Radcliffe, *Place and Field Names of Kirk Bride; Proceedings. I.O.M.N.H.A.S.* IV, 1940-2, 608.

FAIRIES CLIMBING BEARY MOUNTAIN: G. Waldron, op. cit. 104.

3   *Witchcraft; Art-Magic,* pages 41–52

WITCHES IN GAELIC-SPEAKING LANDS: W. W. Gill, *A Second Manx Scrapbook,* 1932, 155.

ABILITY TO CURE FROM A DISTANCE: Joseph Train, *History of the Isle of Man,* 1845, II, 158.

MANANNAN: *Monumenta de Insula Manniae,* I, 1860. J. R. Oliver, *Manx Society,* Vol IV; W. W. Gill, op. cit. II, 433; *Manannan Mac Lir,* J. Vendryes, *Etudes. Celtiques,* VI, 1953-1954.

MANANNAN: Invocation: *William Cashen's Manx Folklore,* 1912, 35. Magic Powers: *Yn Lioar Manninagh,* III, 1902, 135. Magic attributes: P. W. Joyce, *Old Celtic Romances,* 6. Travelling over the sea: J. A. McCulloch, *The Religion of the Ancient Celts,* 1911, 87. Local Ruler: *Little Manannan Son of Leirr, or a Full Account of the Isle of Man,* A. W. Moore, *Manx Ballads and Music,* 1896, 7. Three-legged man: P. W. Joyce, *A Social History of Ancient Ireland,* I, 1903, 259.

CELTIC AFTER-LIFE: J. A. McCulloch, op. cit. 1911, 362-390.

EAMHAIN OF THE APPLES: W. F. Skene, *Celtic Scotland,* 1890, III, 411.

THE DEAD HAND: J. Clague, *Manx Reminiscences,* 1911, 153.

CHURCHYARD MOULD: From oral sources; Also Y.L.M., I, 1889, 190; III, 1902, 379.

SWEARING ON GRAVE: M. A. Mills, *Ancient Ordinances and Statutes of the Isle of Man,* I, 1821, 80; *The Manx Note-Book,* II, 1886, 143.

THE STORY OF GLAM: *Grettis Saga,* 1869, 98-110.
SUNSET FAIRIES: C. Roeder, *Y.L.M.* I, 1889, 327.
TEARE BALLAWHANE: J. Train, op. cit. 1845, II, 161-2.
TEARE'S METHOD OF WORKING: J. Clague, op. cit. 1911, 127.
FAIRIES LEAVING THE ISLAND: J. Train, op. cit. II, 159.
CHILD'S VISIT TO NAN WADE: *Y.L.M.* I, 156; II, 157.
FOLK DOCTORS AND MEDICAL MEN: A. W. Moore, *Further Notes on Manx Folklore,* in *Antiquary,* XXXI, 1895, 295.
MEDICAL BILL PROPOSED AND PARISH PROTEST: *Manx Sun Newspaper,* 24th August, 1844.
1899 MEDICAL BILL: *The Statutes of the Isle of Man,* Vol. VII, 1896-1905, ed. C. T. W. Hughes-Games, 1912.

4   *Witchcraft: The Black Art,* pages 53–66

JONY – WITCH OF KIRK BRADDAN: David Craine, *Manannan's Isle,* 1955, 18.
MANX-GAELIC NAMES FOR WITCHES, AMULETS AND CHARMS: C. C. Roeder, *Manx Notes and Queries,* 1904, 40, 41, 42.
WART CURE: from Oral Source.
HARMFUL USE OF CHARM: J. Clague, *Manx Reminiscences,* 1911, 175.
BURIAL CEREMONY: Blanche Nelson, M. S.c., 1890, *Manx Stories,* Vol. I.
"STRIKING UNKNOWN' A. W. Moore, *Folklore of the Isle of Man,* 1891, 81.
SWEEPING THE ROAD: From personal information.
WITCH REVEALED IN BONFIRE: *Yn Lioar Manninagh,* III, 166.
SACRIFICE: J. Rhys, *Celtic Folklore, Welsh and Manx,* 1901, 305-308.
WITCH TRANSFORMED INTO HARE: S. Baring Gould, *A Book of Folklore,* 45.
SILVER BULLET: J. Clague, op. cit. 169.
HARE EATING GRASS: *Y.L.M.,* III, 164.
'ROUGH UNDER THE FOOT': Story told personally to author.
BREW OF HERBS FOR FORGETFULNESS: A. W. Moore, *Folklore of the Isle of Man,* 1891, 81.
WITCHES' CURSE; WOMEN WISHING ON THEIR KNEES: *Chapter Court Presentments.*
SKEAB LOME: *Chapter Court Presentments,* Patrick, 1735.
ORIGINAL RITUAL OF CURSE: D. Craine, op. cit. 23.
LOO MYNNEY MOLLAGHT: Manx Ballads and Music, ed. A. W. Moore, 1896, *Finn as Oshin,* 2.
THE MANX WITCH: R. E. Brown, *The Collected Poems of T. E. Brown,* 1901, 549.
BEREY DHONE BALLAD: *Manx Ballads and Music,* ed. A. W. Moore, 1896, 73-4.
MAY EVE: William Kennish, *Mona's Isle and Other Poems,* 1844, 'Old May Eve', 48-64.

BERREY DHONE: Identity discussed by W. W. Gill, *A Second Manx Scrapbook*, 1932, 330-7.

ORGANISED WITCH COVENS IN THE ISLE OF MAN: W. W. Gill, op. cit. II, 162-172.

INITIATION OF WITCH: A. W. Moore, *Further Notes on Manx Folklore, Antiquary* **XXXI**, 1895, 296.

SENTENCES PASSED ON WITCHES: *Chapter Court Presentments* (1721-1874).

EXECUTION: D. Craine, op. cit. 1955, 14.

SLIEAU WHALLIAN – WITCH ASSOCIATION: George Woods, *An Account of the Past and Present State of the Isle of Man*, 1811, 159.

ALICE KNAKILL, 1735, *The Manx Note Book*, 1886, **II**, 191.

WITCH AND PEWTER VESSELS: A. W. Moore, op. cit. *Antiquary*, **XXXI**, 1895, 296.

5   *Life and Death,* pages 67–85

FAIRIES A HARMLESS DREAM: John Keble, *Life of Bishop Wilson*, 1863, I, 301.

BAPTISM: *Synodal Ordinances of Bishop Mark, 1291,* Manx Society, Vol. IX, 184; David Craine, *Manannan's Isle*, 1955, 114.

PRECAUTIONS AT BIRTH: A. W. Moore, *Folklore of the Isle of Man*, 1891, 157.

BLITHE MEAT: Hall Caine, *The Deemster*, 1888, 12, 13.

NED LAG Y THURRAN: *Yn Lioar Manninagh*, I, 1889, 76. FAIRY WOMEN: *Y.L.M.* II, 161.

UNBAPTISED CHILD, AND CHILD OF EARY CUSHLIN: *William Cashen's Manx Folklore*, 1912, 5.

NAME-GIVING AND RE-BIRTH OF THE DEAD: Hilda Roderick Ellis, *The Road to Hel*, 1943, 139-47.

FAIRY CHANGELING'S APPEARANCE: *Y.L.M.* III, 1902, 154. *Manx Notes and Queries*, 1904, 56.

CAUL FULL OF BEES: *M.N.&Q.,* 1904, 31.

INFLUENCE OF TIDE: W. Cashen, op. cit. 1912, 6.

USHAG VEG RUY: A. W. Moore, *Manx Ballads and Music*, 1896, 43.

LHONDOO AND USHAG RHEAST: *The Manx Note Book*, II, 1886, 37.

THE STORY OF NJORD AND SKADI: *The Poetic Edda,* Pt. I, 1908, Ed. Olive Bray, 270-1.

SENTENCES OF CHAPTER COURTS – CATHERINE KINRADE: George Waldron, *A Description of the Isle of Man*, 1726, 97 – note 40.

HANDFASTING: David Craine, op. cit. 1955, 141.

COURTING SONGS: A. W. Moore, *Manx Ballads and Music,* 1896, 80, 81, 82, 89, 91.

DOOINNEY – MOYLLEE: A. Cregeen, *A Dictionary of the Manx Language*, 1838.

DOWRY: G. Waldron, op. cit. 59-60.

STATUS OF WOMEN: M. A. Mills, *The Ancient Ordinances and Statutes of the Isle of Man,* 1821, 33, 54, 58.

NO HERRING, NO WEDDING: *Mona Miscellany,* Manx Society, Vol. XXI, 1873, 15.

TRADITIONAL WEDDING CUSTOMS: *M.N.&Q.,* 1904, 34; *Y.L.M.,* III, 1902, 131; J. Clague, *Manx Reminiscences,* 1911, 93, 99; G. Waldron, op. cit., 60.

DIVORCE: D. Craine, op. cit. 1955, 101, 140.

THE STANG: J. Clague, op. cit. 1911, 101.

DEATH SIGNS: A. W. Moore, *FL.I.O.M.,* 1891, 160. *Y.L.M.,* II, 1901, 195; J. Clague, op. cit. 105.

LIGHTS AS SIGNS OF DEATH: S. Baring Gould, *A Book of Folklore,* 31.

SEA CAPTAIN AND DROWNED CREW: *William Sacheverell, An Account of the Isle of Man,* 170, 20.

CORPSE WITH KNOTS AND IRON CROSS: W. Cashen, 20, *Y.L.M.,* III, 1902, 158, 159.

WAKES AND FUNERAL: J. Clague, 107-8; G. Waldron, 61.

6   *The Folk and the Barons,* pages 86–100

FIVE KINGDOMS AT A GLANCE: Local saying.

'WHEN I GO TO THE MOUNT' ETC: Rev. W. Mackenzie, *Stanley Legislation of the Isle of Man, Manx Society,* Vol. III, 1860, 23.

BALLATERSON: J. J. Kneen, *The Place Names of the Isle of Man,* 1925, 280.

GILCOLUM AND ST MAUGHOLD: *The Chronicle of Man and the Sudreys,* I, *Manx Society,* Vol. XXII, 69-75.

STAFF OF ST MAUGHOLD: B. R. S. Megaw. *The Monastery of St Maughold; I.O.M.N.H.A.S. Proceedings,* V, II, 1950, 175.

PARTICLES: A. W. Moore, *History of the Isle of Man,* 1900, I, 345, 346.

EDUCATION: George Waldron, *A Description of the Isle of Man,* 1726, 16.

TITHES AND CHURCH DUES: *Monumenta De Insula Manniae,* Ed. J. R. Oliver, III, *Manx Society,* Vol IX, 1862, 176-190.

NO MANX SERMON: David Craine, *Manannan's Isle,* 1955, 116.

PROVERB: "TA YNSAGH" ETC: A. Cregeen, *A Dictionary of the Manx Language,* 1838, 25.

STRUGGLE BETWEEN BARONS AND LORD OF MAN: M. A. Mills, *The Ancient Ordinances and Statutes of the Isle of Man,* 1821, I, 5, 8, 11, 16-17.

NINETEENTH CENTURY EDITOR: Rev. W. Mackenzie, op. cit., 146, 152, 163, 168, 173.

ANTI-CATHOLIC PUBLIC MEETING IN DOUGLAS: Protestant Protection Society, *Manx Sun,* 7.12.1850, 28.12.1850.

IRISH PRIESTS VISITING KEEILLS: From oral sources.

BLOOD-STOPPING CHARMS: A. W. Moore, *Folklore of the Isle of Man,* 96-8.

HOSPITAL OF BALLACGNIBA: B. R. S. Megaw, *The Barony of St Trinian's in Kirk Marown, J. M. M.* IV, 62, 1940, 175-7.

BOAYL Y SPITAL: J. J. Kneen, *Manx Fairs and Festivals,* *I.O.M.N.H.A.S.,* III, 1925, 68.

BALLAVITCHAL – BALLY-BIATACH: P. W. Joyce *A Social History of Ancient Ireland,* 1903, II, 174.

BARONY OF BANGOR AND SABHAL: *J.M.M.* IV, 60, 1939, 135-8.

TENURE OF THE STRAW: A. W. Moore, op. cit. 1900, II, 875-7.

BAYR NY MAYNAGHYN: J. J. Kneen, op. cit. 1925, 382.

TITHES: Mills, op. cit. I, 102.

RIOTS: A. W. Moore, op. cit. 1900, II, 661-2.

TITHE CORN: Stories heard personally in the 1930s.

BISHOP WILSON AND HIS TENANTS: W. Cubbon, *Gleanings from the Books of the Bishop's Barony, Proceedings. I.O.M.N.H.A.S.,* V, 1946-50, 95.

FAIRIES AT BALLAGLONNEY BRIDGE: Current tradition in the Island.

7   *The Buggane of St Trinian's,* pages 101–106

HISTORICAL BACKGROUND: B. R. S. Megaw, *The Barony of St Trinian's in Marown. J. M. M.* IV, 62, 1940, 175-7.

THE STORY OF THE BUGGANE: William Thwaites, *Isle of Man, its Civil and Ecclesiastical History, Antiquities,* etc, 1863, 353.

BARONS SUMMONED TO DO FEALTY TO SIR JOHN STANLEY: M. A. Mills, The Ancient Ordinances and Statutes of the Isle of Man, 1821, I, 8.

ISLE OF MAN GRANTED TO MONTACUTE: A. W. Moore. *History of the Isle of Man,* 1900, I, 194.

RICHARD DE MANDEVILLE: *The Chronicle of Man and the Sudreys,* I, 1874. *Manx Society,* XXII, 113.

BOG – THE SCLAVE WORD FOR GOD: S. Baring-Gould, *A Book of Folklore,* 85, 86.

"BUGGANE": A. Cregeen, *A Dictionary of the Manx Language,* 1838, 30.

THE DESTRUCTION OF KEEILLS: Stories chiefly from oral sources: Some in H. R. Jenkinson's *Guide to the Isle of Man,* 1878.

STONES TAKEN FROM ST TRINIAN'S: H. R. Jenkinson, *A Smaller Practical Guide to the Isle of Man,* 1878, 53-4.

CLAGH NY KILLEY: H. R. Jenkinson, op. cit. 54.

NORSE LEGENDS ON MANX CROSSES: P. M. C. Kermode, *Traces of the Norse Mythology in the Isle of Man, Y.L.M.,* II, 138-54.

SIGURD STORY: DETAIL ON MANX CROSSES: Hilda Roderick Ellis, *The Story of Sigurd in Viking Art, J.M.M.,* IV, 67, 1942, 87.

8   *The Fairy Cup of Ballafletcher,* pages 107–112

THE STORY OF THE LHIANNAN SHEE OF BALLAFLETCHER: H. R. Oswald, *Vestigia Insulae Manniae Antiquiora,* 1860, *Manx Society,* Vol. V, 189-93.

FORTS BUILT BY MAGNUS: *Chronicle of Man and the Sudreys, Manx Society,* Vol. I, 1874, 141.

DUES AND BENEVOLENCES PAID BY TENANTS OF THE BISHOP'S BARONY: W. Cubbon, *Gleanings from the Books of the Bishop's Barony, Proceedings, I.O.M. N.H.A.S.,* V, II, 1946-50, 91, 97.

PLACE NAME KIRKBY: J. J. Kneen, *The Place Names of the Isle of Man,* 1925, 190.

KING MAGNUS BAREFOOT: Sophia Morrison, *Manx Fairy Tales,* 1929, 177.

OLAF'S SHRINE OPENED BY KING HAROLD: *Chronicle of Man and the Sudreys,* I, *Manx Society,* Vol. XXII, 1874, 153.

DESCRIPTION AND ILLUSTRATION OF THE CUP: Oswald, op. cit. 189, plate, 9. [A somewhat similar drinking glass associated with Ballafletcher and now in the Manx Museum is not considered to be the original glass of the legend.]

THE CUP OF SOMERLED: Walter Scott, *The Lord of the Isles,* Poems, 1909.

9   *Herring Fishermen,* pages 113–128

FISHING SUPERSTITIONS: *William Cashen's Manx Folklore,* 1912, 27-32; Charles Roeder, *Manx Notes and Queries, 1904,* 31, 38, 107-15; John Clague, *Manx Reminiscences,* 1911, 39, 40.

DEEMSTER'S OATH: Joseph Train, *History of the Isle of Man,* 1845, II, 203.

LAWS REGULATING THE FISHING, 1610: M. A. Mills, *The Ancient Ordinances and Statutes of the Isle of Man,* 1821, I, 502.

TYPES OF FISHING BOAT: C. Roeder, op. cit. 107, 111, 112; E. M. Megaw, *Manx Fishing Craft, J.M.M.,* V, 64, 15.

GOOD AND BAD YEARS: M. A. Mills, op. cit. 238-9, *M.N.&Q.,* 1904, 108-148.

BISHOP WILSON'S PRAYER: Rev. John Keble, *The Life of Thomas Wilson, 1863,* I, 175.

WESLEY'S VISIT: *John Wesley and Mann,* Jessie D. Kerruish, *Mannin,* IX, 1917, 515.

FISH TITHE: M. A. Mills, op. cit. 46, 50, 51; *M.N.&Q.,* 1904, 115.

WRECK OF THE HERRING FLEET: Verses: *Mona Miscellany,* Second Series, 1873, *Manx Society,* XXI, 115.

FISHERMEN'S MARCH TO TYNWALD: A. W. Moore, *History of the Isle of Man, 1900,* II, 719.

BEISHT KIONE DHOO: Yn Lioar Manninagh, III, 1902, 142.

HAAF NAMES: C. Roeder, op. cit. 1904, 13, 81, 82, 107, 108.

BOAT SUPPER: W. Cashen, op. cit. 1912, 42; Text of Play, J. Clague op. cit. 1911, 82-91.

10   *Three Places,* pages 129–142

TURF-CUTTING: J. Quine, *The Captain of the Parish,* 1897, 80, 81; B. R. S. Megaw, *The Harvest of the Turbary, J.M.M.* IV, No. 58, 95, 101.

TURF-CUTTING LAWS: *The Ancient Ordinances and Statutes of the Isle of*

Man, M. A. Mills, 1821, 114.

POEM – CUSHAG (JOSEPHINE KERMODE): *Poems,* 1908, 29.

OLD HOUSEHOLD ARTICLES Light: *J.M.M.* VI, 78, 130, 132; Cowree: *J.M.M.,* Thatching; *J.M.M.,* VII, 78, 130, 132.

USES OF HERBS: A. W. Moore, *Folk Medicine in the Isle of Man, Y.L.M.,* III, 1902, 303-16.

SAMPHIRE GATHERERS: J. G. Cumming, *The Isle of Man,* 1848, 149.

LUS NY GRAIH: Christopher Shimmin, *Mannin,* I. II, 1913.

SLOGH NY GABBYL SCREBBAGH: J. J. Kneen, *The Place Names of the Isle of Man,* 1925, 309.

LAW: M. A. Mills, op. cit. 62.

WRECK: M. A. Mills, op. cit. 15.

INFERNAL SPIRIT: *Denton's M.S. Description of the Isle of Man, Y.L.M., Society,* XXL., 350-351; C. Roeder, *M.N.&Q.,* 1904, 65.

CUGHTAGH: W. W. Gill, *A Second Manx Scrap Book 1932,* 252.

SUBMERGED ISLANDS: *Mona Miscellany,* (Second series) 1873, *Manx Society,* XXL, 350-351; C. Roeder, *M.N. & Q.,* 1904, 65.

ST. MICHAEL'S ISLE: J. G. Cumming, op. cit. 91, (note).

TOWN OF SODOR AT LANGNESS: A. W. Moore, *Further Notes on Manx Folklore; Antiquary,* XXXI, 1895, 109.

BISHOP'S VERSES: Scrapbook, Newspaper Cuttings, [Frowde], Manx Museum Library.

ROCKS AT LANGNESS: J. G. Cumming, op. cit. 87.

GHOST OF SAILOR AT LANGNESS: *Y.L.M.,* III, 159.

GHOST ON GRAVE: Oral source.

PIRATE RAID: Kate Dodd, *St Michael's Island and its Neighbourhood,* 13-15.

LAWS – LORD'S GAME: Mills, op. cit. 59, 61.

FALCONS AT CORONATION: *Mannin,* 9, (1917), 524-6.

"SHAWK": P. G. Ralfe, *The Birds of the Isle of Man, 1905,* 130, 132.

11   *Smugglers' and other Tales,* pages 000-000

HISTORICAL AND LEGAL BACKGROUND: Rupert Jarvis, *Illicit Trade with the Isle of Man,* 1671-1765; *Transactions of Lancashire and Cheshire Antiquarian Society,* 1945-6, 245-261; G. Waldron, op. cit. 9, 88 (note 22).

QUILLIAM: Christopher Shimmin, *The Smuggler, Mannin* I, no. I, 1913, 48.

STORIES ABOUT THE BOAT "MODDEY DHOO": A. E. Lamothe, *Manx Yarns,* 1905, 163, 164.

ACTS TO CONTROL SMUGGLING: M. A. Mills, *The Ancient Ordinances and Statutes of the Isle of Man,* 1821, I, 131, 508, 509.

PHANTOM COACH – MALEW: W. W. Gill, *A Manx Scrapbook* 1929, 343.

COACH–PORT ST MARY: C. Roeder, *M.N.&Q.,* 58.

GOODS FROM WRECK HIDDEN IN TOMB IN MAUGHOLD

CHURCHYARD: *Manx Sun;* 2.4.1842.

LANDING AT BALLAUGH BURN-FOOT: P. W. Caine, *Proceedings. I.O.M.N.H.A.S.*, IV, 1938, 293.

SMUGGLING BETWEEN ISLE OF MAN AND KIRKCUDBRIGHTSHIRE, THE MANXMEN'S LAKE: Walter Scott, *Guy Mannering*, Everyman Edition, 425, 426.

OOIG NY SEYIR. *W. Cashen's Manx Folklore*, 18.

FAIRY CARPENTERS MAKING COFFINS: W. W. Gill, *A Third Manx Scrapbook*, 1963, 36.

THE ORIGINAL STORY OF THE MODDEY DHOO IN PEEL CASTLE: George Waldron, op. cit. 1706, 12, 13. The Duchess of Gloucester is supposed to have been imprisoned in the dungeon of Peel Castle (see Shakespeare's Henry VI, Act II, Part 2, Scene III, in which she is banished to the Isle of Man).

STORIES OF THE UNDERGROUND CHAMBER IN CASTLE RUSHEN: George Waldron, op. cit.

THE DEVIL'S DEN: George Waldron, op. cit. 68.

CRONUS IMPRISONED IN AN ISLAND: Lewis Spence, *The Magic Arts in Celtic Britain*, 1945, 152, 153, 154.

WRECKERS ON BALLURE SHORE: Hall Caine, *The Manxman*, 1897,
THE CARRAS DHOO MEN: Esther Nelson, *A Legend of the Isle,* in *Island Minstrelsy* 1837, 73-83.

12   *The Farmer and his Friends,* pages 156–163
CRITIC OF MANX FARMERS: Thomas Quayle, *A General View of the Agriculture of the Isle of Man*, 1812, 20.

LIFE IN CREGNEASH: Edward Faragher, *A Sketch of Old Cregneash*, *J.M.M.*, III, 189-91.

GOLD ON THE CUSHAGS: Local saying.

INCIDENT AT TYNWALD FAIR– From *The People and Hewitts Journal*, *1840* (Historical Sketches Scrapbook in Manx Museum).

STORIES OF BEGGARS: From personal knowledge.

FYNNODEREE, GLASHEN, DOOINNEY OIE: Discussion of them in J. Rhys' *Celtic Folklore, Welsh and Manx*, 1901, I, 323-353.

STORY OF FYNNODEREE GATHERING THE SHEEP, AND ANALYSIS OF HIS ANCESTRY: I. M. Killip, *The Fynnoderee and the Li'l Loghtan*, *J.M.M.*, VII, 83, 1967, 58-61; Alfred Nutt, *Studies in the Legend of the Holy Grail*.

ROMANTIC VERSION OF THE FYNNODEREE STORY: Edward Callow, *The Fynnoderee and other Legends of the Isle of Man*, 1882, 2.

THE URUISG: *Transactions of the Gaelic Society of Inverness*, XXX, 1924, 38.

STORY BY JOHN BUCHAN: *No Man's Land* in the collection of stories, *The Watcher by the Threshold*.

13   *Hollantide to Harvest,* pages 164–179

THE CELTIC NEW YEAR: Marie-Louise Sjoestedt, *Gods and Heroes of the Celts*, Translated by Miles Dillon, 1949, 47-56.

MANX HOLLANTIDE CUSTOMS: C. I. Paton, *Manx Calendar Customs*, 1939, 52, 54, (sacrifice, footnote), 191; C. Roeder, *Contributions to the Folklore of the Isle of Man, Yn Lioar Manninagh*, III, 1902, 184-6, 290; A. W. Moore, *Folklore of the Isle of Man*, 1891, 123-6, (Soddag Valloo 123). J. Rhys, *Celtic Folklore. Welsh and Manx*, 1901, 315-20.

SALT – MANUFACTURE: P. W. Joyce, *A Social History of Ancient Ireland*, 1903, II, 135.

SPINNING PROVERB: *Journal of the Manx Museum*, VI, 81, 1965, 228.

WORDSWORTH: *Song for the Spinning Wheel*, Poems, 1897, 406.

CANDLES, RUSHLIGHTS: I. M. Killip, *The Light of Other Days*, *J.M.M.*, VI, 1961-62, 130.

ARNANE: A. Cregeen, *A Dictionary of the Manx Language*, 1838, 20.

WEATHER LORE AND SAYINGS: C. I. Paton, op. cit. 1939, 62, 179, 188, 194.

CAILLAGH NY GUESHAG: *Y.L.M.*, I, 223.

MAY EVE AND MAY DAY CUSTOMS: Joseph Train, *History of the Isle of Man*, 1845, II, 117-118; C. I. Paton, op. cit. 278-287; *Diary of Caesar Wattleworth* (1791-1805), Extracts in *J. M. M.* VI, 80, 1964, 221, 222.

THARREY: A. Cregeen, op. cit. 167.

HARVEST CUSTOMS, THE MHEILLEA: William Kennish, *Mona's Isle and Other Poems*, 1844, 27; Joseph Train, op. cit 122.

CORN SPIRIT: J. G. Frazer, *The Golden Bough*, Abridged Edition, 563.

LAA LUANYS: C. I. Paton, op. cit. 45-48. J. Clague, *Manx Reminiscences*, 1911, 81.

CHURCH'S DISAPPROVAL: Lonan Chapter Court Presentments, 1732.

"LIKE TO THE SETTING SUN" ETC: P. W. Joyce, *Old Celtic Romances*, 1907, 38.

CROM DUBH AND LUGH: Maire MacNeill, *The Festival of Lughnasa*, 1962, 416, 429.

JEPHTHA'S DAUGHTER: J. Rhys, *Celtic Folklore Welsh and Manx*, I, 1901, 313; C. I. Paton, op. cit. 47.

WELL WORSHIP, CHIBBYR BELTAIN: W. W. Gill, *A Second Manx Scrapbook*, 1929, 68.

14   *Old Christmas and the Oie'll Voirrey*, pages 180–187

THE METHODIST ATTITUDE: *The Manx Conference Book of Minutes*, 1780-8, 12, 20, 75, 78.

JOHN WESLEY AND THE MANX LANGUAGE: *John Wesley and Mann*, Jessie D. Kerruish, *Mannin*, IX, 1917, 516.

THE OIE'L VOIRREY: Hall Caine, *Old Manx Customs, Liverpool Mercury*, 22.10.1888.

CARVALS QUOTED: *Carvalyn Ghailchagh*, (Manx Carols), 1891, 236-8 (on Bad Women); Verses from other Carvals, 31, 147, 135.

THE DISPUTE BETWEEN BODY AND SOUL: C. I. Paton, *Manx Carvals and Carval Books, with notes on some of the MSS. Proceedings. I.O.M.N.H.A.S.*, *II*, 1925, 497.

OIE'L VOIRREY CUSTOMS: *Y.L.M.*, III, 190, *M.N.&Q.*, 17; A. W. Moore, *Folklore of the Isle of Man*, 127-128.

MANX CHRISTMAS CUSTOMS: C. I. Paton, *Manx Calendar Customs*, 1939, 63, ff; G. Waldron, *A Description of the Isle of Man*, 1726, 50.

HUNT THE WREN: J. Clague, *Manx Reminiscences* 1911, 13; G. Waldron, op. cit. 49.

BRONZE AGE DERIVATION. *The Folklore of Birds*, E. A. Armstrong, 1958, 166.

OLD CHRISTMAS DAY; STORY OF THE FLAX, WATCHING THE MYRRH: C. I. Paton. op. cit. 120, 121, 179, ff., *Y.L.M.*, III, 189-91.

Select Bibliography

William Cashen's Manx Folklore, 1912
JOHN CLAGUE, *Manx Reminiscences*, 1911
DAVID CRAINE, *Manannan's Isle*, 1955
J. G. CUMMINGS. *The Isle of Man*. 1848
CUSHAG, (JOSEPHINE KERMODE) *Poems, 1912*
W. W. GILL. A *First, Second* and *Third Manx Scrapbook*. 1929, 1932, 1963
RUPERT C. JARVIS. *Illicit Trade with the Isle of Man. 1671–1765*. In the Transactions of the Lancashire and Cheshire Antiquarian Society, 1945–1946
H. R. JENKINSON. *A Smaller Practical Guide to the Isle of Man*. 1878
P. W. JOYCE. *A Social History of Ancient Ireland*. 1903
WILLIAM KENNISH. *Mona's Isle and Other Poems*. 1844
P. M. C. KERMODE. *Traces of the Norse Mythology in the Isle of Man*. Y. L. M. II. 1901
JESSIE D. KERRUISH. *John Wesley and Mann*. Mannin IX. 1917
J. J. KNEEN. *The Place Names of the Isle of Man*. 1925
MAIRE MACNEILL *The Festival of Lughnasa*. 1962.
B. R. S. MEGAW. *The Barony of St Trinian's in Kirk Marown*. J. M. M. 1940
M. A. MILLS. *The Ancient Ordinances and Statutes of the Isle of Man*. I. 1821
A. W. MOORE. *Folklore of the Isle of Man*. 1891
  Manx Ballads and Music. 1896
  History of the Isle of Man 1900
SOPHIA MORRISON. *Manx Fairy Tales*. 1929
J. A. MUCULLOCK. *The Religion of the Ancient Celts*. 1911
ESTHER NELSON. *Island Minstrelsy*. 1837
H. R. OSWALD. *Vestigia Insulae Manniae Antiquiora*. Manx Society. V. 1860
C. I. PATON. *Manx Calendar Customs*. Folklore 1939
CHARLES ROEDER. *Manx Notes and Queries*. 1904
  Contributions to the Folklore of the South of the Isle of Man. Y. L. M. III. 1896.
J. RHYS. *Celtic Folklore, Welsh and Manx*. 1901
LEWIS SPENCE. *The Magic Arts in Celtic Britain*. 1945
WILLIAM THWAITES. *The Isle of Man, its Civil and Ecclesiastical History and Antiquities*. 1863
JOSEPH TRAIN. *History of the Isle of Man*. 1845
GEORGE WALDRON. *A Description of the Isle of Man*, Manx Society XI.

Index of Tale Types

Folktales have been classified on an international system based on their plots, devised by Antti Aarne and Stith Thompson in *The Types of the Folktale*, 1961; numbers from this system are preceded by the letters AT. Some local legends were classified by R.Th. Christiansen in *The Migratory Legends*, 1958, and his system was further developed by K. M. Briggs in *A Dictionary of British Folktales*, 1970-1; these numbers are preceded by ML, and the latter also by an asterisk.

Motif Index

A motif is an element which occurs within the plot of one or several folktales (e.g. 'cruel stepmother'). They have been classified thematically in Stith Thompson's *Motif Index of Folk Literature*, 1966: the numbers below are taken from this, together with B. Baughman's *Type and Motif Index of the Folktales of England and North America*, 1966.

General Index